NEW WINE

GW00469471

About the author:

Mel B., a recovering alcoholic, has written numerous articles and essays on the subject of Twelve Step programs. He is a retired business writer and has lived in Toledo, Ohio, since 1972, where he edits a monthly senior citizens section for a weekly newspaper group and contributes occasional articles to the daily newspaper, *The Blade*. Born in Norfolk, Nebraska, he served in the United States Navy in the Pacific during World War II and later lived and worked for many years in Jackson, Michigan. He and his wife, Lori, a fashion illustrator for a Toledo department store group, have four grown children and three grandchildren.

2015.

NEW WINE

The Spiritual Roots of The Twelve Step Miracle

Mel B.

 HAZELDEN®

First published October 1991.

ISBN: 0-89486-772-5

Library of Congress Catalog Card Number: 91-73799

Printed in the United States of America.

Editor's notes:
  Hazelden Educational Materials offers a variety of information on chemical dependency and related areas. Our publications do not necessarily represent Hazelden's programs, nor
do they officially speak for any Twelve Step organization.
  The Twelve Steps and Twelve Traditions are reprinted and
adapted with permission of Alcoholics Anonymous World
Services, Inc. Permission to reprint and adapt the Twelve Steps
does not mean that AA has reviewed or approved the contents
of this publication, nor that AA agrees with the views expressed
herein. The views expressed herein are solely those of the
author. AA is a program of recovery from alcoholism—use of
the Twelve Steps in connection with programs and activities
which are patterned after AA, but which address other
problems, does not imply otherwise.
  All quotes from *The AA Grapevine* are reprinted by permission of AA Grapevine, Inc.

For Lori

Contents

Acknowledgments

Writers, unlike people in other commercial ventures, always have numerous allies who freely offer their assistance and advice without compensation. It is always pleasant to acknowledge this generous assistance and to note the satisfaction these kind people have when they see the results of their advice in print.

I have always been particularly grateful for professionals in public libraries, who have been unfailingly cooperative and cheerful when I've requested research help. For this project, I received generous cooperation at the Toledo/Lucas County Public Library from Don Barnette, Cathy Beery, Ernie Brown, Greg Brown, Brian Nichols, and Anthony Schafer.

I'm also indebted to Frank Mauser at the AA Archives in New York City, and to Nell Wing, Mr. Mauser's predecessor, who schooled me on AA history and the life of Bill Wilson. Naomi Strassberg of *The AA Grapevine* staff was especially helpful; Bob P., the former general manager at AA World Services, kindly responded to a review of his comments.

Bill Pittman generously sent me more than thirty books relating to the Oxford Group and other subjects.

The major contributor of information, whose name appears frequently in the narrative, was T. Willard Hunter. It has been largely through Mr. Hunter's efforts that publishers are now beginning to acknowledge the role of Frank Buchman in the ever-growing mutual, spiritual self-help movements. Through Mr. Hunter, I also became acquainted with James Newton, who had an important supporting role in the events that led to the founding of Alcoholics Anonymous.

Other persons who have been helpful or supportive during the preparation of this book include Salvation Army Major William Bode, Richard Crook, Teresa Green, Margaret and Mark Guldseth, Bill Jones, June and John Kinnecom, Ernest Kurtz, John Lester, Katherine McCarthy, Marion Orr, Dorothy

Seiberling, former Congressman John F. Seiberling, Sherre Smith, Melanie Solberg, Salvation Army Captain Tom Taylor, Alice Watson, and Sue Smith Windows.

I also wish to express gratitude for the support and encouragement of my editor at Hazelden and his associates.

While I've had many helpful allies in this project, all responsibility for any errors is entirely my own.

*But new wine must be put
into fresh wineskins.*

— Luke 5:38

Introduction—
What Do AA Members Believe?

Since 1935, the fellowship of Alcoholics Anonymous has expressed an advanced spiritual approach to solving human problems.

This spiritual expression was lightly felt at first, because it took the tiny society four years to bring together one hundred members. This was the number of alcoholics who were recovering in the fellowship by 1939, when the society published its book *Alcoholics Anonymous*. This basic text also gave the fellowship its name.

The AA society traces its beginnings to a May 1935 meeting of two men in Akron, Ohio. Bill Wilson, a stockbroker from New York, had recovered from alcoholism some months earlier with help from the Oxford Group, a spiritual fellowship. Facing a difficult weekend following a business setback, he sought out another alcoholic to help—a practice that had strengthened his own sobriety in previous months. The person he found, an Akron surgeon named Dr. Bob Smith, became his partner in launching Alcoholics Anonymous. Both men are now deceased—Smith died in 1950 and Wilson in 1971.[1]

Word about AA started getting around after release of the book in 1939, and by early 1941, AA had more than a thousand members. This membership quadrupled in a matter of months with the publication early that year of a well-written, laudatory article in *The Saturday Evening Post*, then one of America's most popular family magazines. AA's growth has been steady ever since, and the fellowship entered the 1990s with nearly two million members worldwide. AA has also inspired the formation of numerous other "Anonymous" societies that deal with a wide spectrum of human problems. Most of these societies also use AA's famous Twelve Steps, first published in the book *Alcoholics Anonymous*, and Twelve

1

Traditions, which were added in the second edition. This book is now in its third edition and has reportedly sold more than ten million copies worldwide, including many translations into other languages.

AA's remarkable continuing success, as well as the expansion of groups applying the Twelve Steps to problem areas other than alcoholism, has drawn increasing public attention over the years. Early on, virtually all comment about AA was in the form of lavish praise. Later, in the 1960s, critical magazine articles began to appear. As the society matured even further, some professionals in the health and behavioral sciences would express some misgivings about AA's philosophy and methods while praising its results. It also was generally accepted, at least by many professionals, that AA was largely successful because of its group support—people banding together with a common purpose.

Ask an AA member why the program works, however, and you often get an answer that has religious overtones. An AA member is likely to attribute his or her recovery to the help of a Higher Power as well as the group. In most meeting discussions, AA members frequently express gratitude to a Higher Power (or, as worded in Steps Three and Eleven, *God as we understood Him*). This can sometimes be very close to the kind of sentiments that are heard at an evangelical revival meeting. While an AA group discussion might also be sprinkled with some profanity, the frequent references to a Higher Power still display what are usually looked upon as religious feelings.

When AA members talk this way, they're carrying on in a tradition that comes straight from their revered founders, Bill Wilson and Dr. Bob Smith. "The central fact of our lives today is the absolute certainty that our Creator has entered into our hearts and lives in a way which is indeed miraculous," Wilson wrote in 1939. "He has commenced to accomplish those things for us which we could never do by ourselves."[2] Dr. Bob Smith, adding to this same thought, wrote to the still-suffering alcoholics, "Your Heavenly Father will never let you down!"[3]

Along with expressing religious feelings, Wilson and other AA members also freely acknowledged that AA's spiritual principles have their source in traditional religious beliefs—"the common property of mankind," Wilson called them. But he was always quick to add that AA was *not* a religion. Under no circumstances must the fellowship get into competition with religion, he told AA members at their International Conference in 1955. "If we appeared to be a new religious sect, we would certainly be in trouble.... So we began to emphasize the fact that AA was a way of life that conflicted with no one's religious belief."[4]

But how could a fellowship use what seemed to be religious language without being labeled a religion? The answer is partly in the frequent use of the word *spiritual*. AA is a spiritual fellowship, not a religion, its members insist. This special care to define the fellowship as a spiritual society rather than a religious one has helped it escape being branded as a cult.

This was no small achievement and one that is all the more impressive to anybody who has traced the course of religious development in America. Virtually no group that began outside established churches and temples and that was organized around a God-centered program has ever been able to survive without finally being viewed as yet another religious sect. The Oxford Group, the society from which AA evolved, had some success in bridging religious barriers, but it eventually came to be seen and judged as a distinct religious sect. It was attacked not only by religious conservatives, but also by the modernists, who should have liked its program. The New Thought groups of the nineteenth century had the laudable goal of defining spiritual ideals for all churches, but they too are considered separate religious sects today. Even The Salvation Army, surely one of the most universally approved religious organizations, has firm doctrines that occasionally bring it into mild controversy.

Besides its emphasis on spirituality rather than religious doctrine, AA may have successfully sidestepped sectarian issues

3

for still another reason: its singleness of purpose, which is only
to help the alcoholic who still suffers and to aid its members
in maintaining sobriety. As for defining what any member's
relationship to the Higher Power might be, AA headed off
trouble simply by leaving any conception of God up to the individual. Though few religious organizations seem to be able
to do this and still preserve their identity, it seems to work in
AA. In addition—and probably another reason AA has mostly
avoided religious controversy—its members are encouraged to
hold on to any religious beliefs they may already have.

Though AA denies that it holds any views about the nature
of God, this statement from AA's basic text, the Big Book, comes
as close as anything to defining the fellowship's understanding
of Spirit:

> As soon as we admitted the possible existence of a
> Creative Intelligence, a Spirit of the Universe under-
> lying the totality of things, we began to be possessed
> by a new sense of power and direction, provided we
> took other simple steps. We found that God does not
> make too hard terms with those who seek Him. To us,
> the Realm of Spirit is broad, roomy, all inclusive; never
> exclusive or forbidding to those who earnestly seek.
> It is open, we believe, to all men.[5]

This very optimistic and fair-minded statement may appeal
to some religious people. But it's not the sort of description
that could survive very long in an arena of intense discussion
among most traditional religious thinkers. For one thing, many
theologians would probably condemn it as being too general,
and would ask what it has to say about specific religious doctrines. And some doctrinaire religious believers doubt very
much that the Spiritual Realm is open to everybody; wars have
been fought over this single point.

But AA went no further than this in defining what it meant
by "Spirit," and never insisted that even this was the end of
the matter. This open-minded, conciliatory approach headed

off arguments before they ever started. AA members have always issued disclaimers when discussing God: Typical is, "Our program is spiritual, not religious." If pressed for what the program's actual definition of *spiritual* is, however, it's doubtful that many AA members could explain.

There are practical definitions, however, that can be interpolated from patterns of spiritual expression in the lives of members as AA evolved. A great majority of people in AA probably still accept the Big Book's presentation of Spirit as a Guiding Power present throughout the Universe and also in the individual and any group of people. This Spirit is likely to be thought of as benign rather than punitive, immediately available rather than remote, and personal as well as universal. These AA members' Higher Power is perhaps somewhat as Tennyson expressed it: "Speak to Him thou for He hears, and Spirit with Spirit can meet—closer is He than breathing, and nearer than hands and feet."

"Closer than breathing" is also very close to many AA members' ideas of Spirit, which, after all, comes from the root word for breath. Emmet Fox, a writer and popular New York minister of the 1930s and 1940s who influenced the pioneering AAs, described this Spiritual Power as "something that surrounds us as the atmosphere does."[6] Spirit is not literally the air of the physical atmosphere, of course. But the atmosphere's function in preserving life is a useful analogy for conceptualizing how Spirit works.

This large segment of AA members also share the belief that this Higher Power is accessible to any person—"does not make too hard terms" for seekers. This is an extremely important point for many suffering alcoholics who arrive at AA's door with a heavy burden of guilt. In spite of what any person has done, a Higher Power is immediately available to support him or her in finding sobriety and full recovery. The "simple steps" required of the alcoholic are admission of helplessness (Step One), willingness to seek God's help (Steps Two and Three), a self-inventory (Steps Four through Seven), and efforts at restitution for wrongs done (Steps Eight through Ten).

There is considerable emphasis, too, on *maintaining* one's relationship with a Higher Power. In this connection, two terms that come up frequently in AA discussions are *humility* and *gratitude*. The relationship with a Higher Power is called a "conscious contact with God *as we understood Him*'' (Step Eleven), and most AA members tend to believe that this "conscious contact" is immediately lost if one again becomes prideful, egotistical, or selfish (Step Twelve).

Though it had previously been used as a collection of principles, AA's spiritual program was written by Bill Wilson as the Twelve Steps in 1938 and published in the Big Book in 1939. These steps outline the spiritual program for the individual alcoholic. Later on, other spiritual principles were prepared as the Twelve Traditions and accepted by the fellowship in 1950 at its first international conference. Published in *Twelve Steps and Twelve Traditions* in 1953 and reprinted in the second edition of the Big Book in 1955, they outline the spiritual program for AA as a society.

At the same time, AA acquired other principles that are offered in the form of cherished slogans and sayings. What came to be known as the Serenity Prayer is from a prayer written by theologian Reinhold Niebuhr, who probably drew from earlier sources. It was adopted by the fellowship very early on and has acquired significant meaning to members.

For much of its spiritual program, AA owes a great debt to the Oxford Group and, it follows, to Oxford Group founder Frank Buchman, as additional chapters in this book will show. It's important to remember, however, that AA has acquired a spiritual character of its own since separating from the Oxford Group more than fifty years ago. At the same time, AA relies on valuable insights that its founders received from the medical profession. The Oxford Group, although successful in helping a number of alcoholics, never had AA's sharp-focused view of alcoholism as a physical and mental disease, as well as a sickness of the Spirit.

The result of such development is that AA today is very much a "synthetic" program. In a study of alcoholism published in 1985, Doctors Jack H. Mendelson and Nancy K. Mello asserted that the strengths and weaknesses of AA might be abstracted from the life story of Bill Wilson. Referring to the AA founder as its "charismatic leader," they wrote, "The building blocks that Bill W. synthesized into his concept of a fellowship that could help alcoholics were derived from disparate sources: the psychology of Carl Jung, transcendental and existential mysticism, Christian fundamentalism and early notions from American medicine about the role of allergy as a cause of alcoholism."[7]

Bill Wilson also used the idea of AA as a synthetic program. Speaking at the Yale (University) Summer Studies on Alcohol in 1944, he said that he and the early AA pioneers had been influenced by Dr. Alexis Carrel's argument for synthesis, and this had become part of the AA system. In *Man the Unknown,* published in 1935, Carrel had noted the need for synthesis of knowledge from several sciences for the remaking or advancement of humankind.[8] This synthesis, as Wilson interpreted it from Carrel's writings, would mean taking several existing ideas and blending them into something new that would be of service to troubled alcoholics. In shaping AA, the always-practical Wilson was prepared to use building blocks from any source, the only proviso being that they had to work and be something a troubled alcoholic would accept.

The term "spiritual" fell perfectly in line with Wilson's overriding objective of helping the sick alcoholic. Spirit, like the atmosphere, conveys the idea of a Presence that is available to anybody for beneficial purposes. It could work for anybody willing to accept it. Moreover, it enabled Wilson to borrow freely from many sources without taking on any additional political and religious baggage that might get in the way of helping alcoholics.

True to Wilson's statement that AA's spiritual principles are "the common property of mankind," AA's General Service

Office in New York City is generous and responsive in permitting almost anybody who wishes to adopt these ideas for another type of fellowship. Most of the new fellowships use both the AA Steps and Traditions, usually noting that permission has been granted by AA headquarters. AA does not affiliate with any person or organization, but it does cooperate graciously and spontaneously with almost everybody.

If AA's principles are "the common property of mankind," however, how did they eventually come to be used by AA? What did AA do with these principles to make them effective in helping alcoholics, when so many had failed in the past? If the principles are indeed "ancient," why haven't more people benefited from them in past centuries? What is it about AA that keeps the fellowship from drifting off into other ventures that would weaken it in carrying out its single purpose of helping alcoholics?

These questions will be taken up in the next chapters in tracing the spiritual roots of the Twelve Steps. It will be shown that AA's great spiritual ideas are all traceable to ancient religious ideas, primarily as they were expressed in the Christian religions but also traceable to fundamental teachings in other world religions and philosophies. There is really nothing in AA that hasn't been known and taught for centuries and could not have been immediately available to anybody who wanted to put the principles into practice. Indeed, at various times, people have used the same principles in a variety of ways, and always with success in finding "conscious contact" with God as they understood God. What's important today, however, is how AA found this "new wine of the Spirit" and put it to uses that are producing ever-widening circles of goodwill, friendship, and recovery in the world.

CHAPTER ONE

An Overdue Letter to Dr. Carl Jung

Nobody really knows today why AA co-founder Bill Wilson finally reached a decision, in January 1961, to write to the eminent Swiss psychologist and psychiatrist Carl Gustav Jung.

It was a decision long in the making. According to Nell Wing, Bill's secretary for twenty years (and later the AA archivist), Bill had first considered writing to Jung in late 1945, at the suggestion of a Jungian student. This was six years after Jung's indirect but important contribution to AA's founding had been noted in the first edition of the Big Book, *Alcoholics Anonymous.* The idea of writing to Jung came up from time to time in the next fifteen years, without any action ever being taken.

Bill Wilson finally made the decision at a time when he keenly felt the years slipping away. He had turned sixty-five the previous November, and he still had self-imposed assignments he wanted to complete in his special role as an "elder statesman" of AA. These uncompleted tasks were much on his mind as he took long walks over the wooded slopes around his home near Bedford Hills, New York, where he and his wife, Lois, had lived since 1941. At other times, he sat at his desk in "Wit's End," the small den he and a friend had constructed in the woods behind the house, and scribbled ideas on yellow legal pads.

These thoughts sometimes emerged as lengthy letters or manuscripts, which he then delivered to Nell Wing to type as first drafts that might later be amended several times before mailing. Where AA was concerned, Bill Wilson did nothing lightly. If there was ever a man who took extreme care in preparing the letters he finally mailed, it was Bill Wilson. His obsessive concern was to avoid even a single word that would bring discredit upon AA or create problems for alcoholics seeking recovery.

The decision to write to Jung, when it finally came, was an example of perfect timing. In hindsight, it seems to be further proof of *synchronicity*—Jung's term for two or more simultaneously occurring events that exhibit a significant, meaningful, yet noncausal, relationship. Bill Wilson, whose entire life had been changed by miraculous events that had the surface appearances of chance or random occurrences, would have bought the idea of synchronicity. (But Wilson, always self-conscious about appearing to palm off anything that bordered on the intellectual, might have warned that synchronicity was a "ten-dollar word" before offering it to AA members!)

Whether ordained by chance or by a Higher Coordinating Power, the timing couldn't have been better. In slightly more than four months, Jung would be dead just short of reaching his eighty-sixth birthday. He was failing in January, but the letter reached him at a time when he could still prepare a brief but profound response that added new support to AA's view of its spiritual program. Jung's reply was judged so important to AA that it has been reprinted several times in the society's publication, *The AA Grapevine,* and has come to be quoted as a valuable endorsement. It has become a part of AA literature, like the Serenity Prayer and other useful tools that came from sources outside the fellowship.

Bill's letter of January 23, 1961, to Jung was comprehensive. He introduced himself as an AA co-founder writing a long-overdue letter of appreciation. He went on to explain how his own sobriety had resulted from Jung's work with an alcoholic named Rowland H. in 1931. (Surprisingly, Bill misspelled the name as "Roland," despite the fact that both he and the highly competent Nell Wing had access to information providing the correct spelling!) Bill described how Jung had first told Rowland that his alcoholic condition was hopeless. "Coming from you, one he so trusted and admired, the impact upon him was immense," Bill recalled.

But then, Bill went on to write, Jung had told Rowland that there might be some hope, "provided he could become the subject of a spiritual or religious experience—in short, a genuine conversion. You pointed out how such an experience, if brought about, might remotivate him when nothing else could. But you did caution, though, that while such experiences had sometimes brought recovery to alcoholics, they were, nevertheless, comparatively rare. You recommended that he place himself in a religious atmosphere and hope for the best. This I believe was the substance of your advice."[1]

Bill then told Jung about the favorable outcome this advice had produced. First, Rowland had found his recovery in a fellowship called the Oxford Group, an evangelical movement then at the height of success in Europe and North America. In New York City, Rowland had become associated with Calvary Church, whose rector, Dr. Sam Shoemaker, was an Oxford Group leader. Rowland's work with alcoholics presently led him to Edwin T., the "Ebby" who carried the message to Bill Wilson in late 1934. Bill told how he had found his own recovery in the aftermath of an amazing spiritual experience, and how the vision of a society of alcoholics helping each other had then come out of this. He also explained what AA had become by 1961 and sent along to Jung the books *Alcoholics Anonymous* and *Alcoholics Anonymous Comes of Age.* Expressing his own interest in Jung's work, and particularly an introduction Jung had once authored for a translation of the ancient Chinese text titled *I Ching,* Bill closed by saying, "Please be certain that your place in the affection, and in the history, of our Fellowship, is like no other."[2]

Jung responded immediately. His letter, dated January 30, 1961, follows on the next page.

Dear Mr. Wilson:

Your letter has been very welcome indeed.

I had no news from Rowland H. any more and often wondered what has been his fate. Our conversation which he has adequately reported to you had an aspect of which he did not know. The reason that I could not tell him everything was that those days I had to be exceedingly careful of what I said. I had found out that I was misunderstood in every possible way. Thus I was very careful when I talked to Rowland H. But what I really thought about, was the result of many experiences with men of his kind.

His craving for alcohol was the equivalent, on a low level, of the spiritual thirst of our being for wholeness, expressed in medieval language: the union with God.

How could one formulate such an insight in a language that is not misunderstood in our days?

The only right and legitimate way to such an experience is, that it happens to you in reality and it can only happen to you when you walk on a path which leads you to higher understanding. You might be led to that goal by an act of grace or through a personal and honest contact with friends, or through a higher education of the mind beyond the confines of mere rationalism. I see from your letter that Rowland H. has chosen the second way, which was, under the circumstances, obviously the best one.

I am strongly convinced that the evil principle prevailing in this world leads the unrecognized spiritual need into perdition, if it is not counteracted either by real religious insight or by the protective wall of human community. An ordinary man, not protected by an action from above and isolated in society, cannot resist the power of evil, which is called very aptly the Devil. But the use of such words arouses so many mistakes that one can only keep aloof from them as much as possible.

These are the reasons why I could not give a full and

sufficient explanation to Rowland H. But I am risking it with you because I conclude from your very decent and honest letter that you have acquired a point of view above the misleading platitudes one usually hears about alcoholism.

You see, alcohol in Latin is <u>spiritus</u> and you use the same word for the highest religious experience as well as for the most depraving poison. The helpful formula therefore is: <u>spiritus contra spiritum</u>.

Thanking you again for your kind letter.

I remain
yours sincerely

C. G. Jung[3]

Jung, whose love for Latin terms and biblical quotations is represented on his gravestone, added Psalm 42:1 as a footnote: "As the hart panteth after the water brooks, so panteth my soul after thee, O God." A figurative translation of his Latin formula is, "It takes the Spirit of God to overcome the (harmful) spirit of alcohol."

Delighted with Jung's quick response, Bill Wilson immediately sent off an additional letter. But there was no reply, and Jung died on June 6, 1961, at his home on the shore of his beloved Lake Zurich in Kusnacht, Switzerland.

(Bill later described Jung's letter, which he said looked as if it had been tapped out on a typewriter with one finger, "as one of my most cherished possessions."[4] Bill's wife, Lois, framed the letter and kept it on a wall at their home, Stepping Stones, in Bedford Hills, New York.)

Jung's letter, though important to Bill Wilson and AA members, was nothing more than a fragment in Jung's total output of books and other papers. These writings had established his great reputation and gave him ranking with Sigmund Freud and Alfred Adler as a founder of modern psychotherapy. But none of this really had any direct role in the development of AA. What mattered most, for AA purposes, was that Jung had encouraged Rowland H. to seek a religious conversion as a possible solution to his drinking problem.

As far as is known, Jung did not outline where such an experience might be found, and nobody really knows what put Rowland H. in touch with the Oxford Group, where he found his answer. But Jung's advice gave motion to a process that is not unlike the continuous passing of a lighted torch by a series of relay runners. If Rowland had not found such a solution for himself, he would not have recovered so that he was able to aid Ebby T., who would carry the Oxford Group message to Bill Wilson in 1934. And if sobriety had not found its way to Bill Wilson, it's hard to see how there could have been an AA movement as we know it today. Anybody who has studied the early development of AA must acknowledge Wilson's key role as indispensable, although others certainly made important contributions. Imagining AA without Bill Wilson is like thinking of Stradivarius violins without Stradivarius.

It was also fortunate that Rowland sought help directly from Carl Jung, and not one of the other great psychiatrists he might have consulted in Europe in 1931. Howard T., an early AA member from Detroit, used to say in his talks that Rowland had initially tried to make an appointment with Sigmund Freud in Vienna, and had gone to Jung only as a second choice. It is logical that Rowland's first choice would have been Freud, the founder of psychoanalysis, who at that time had already influenced an entire generation of American psychiatrists and psychologists. But the early 1930s were troubled years for Freud, who had suffered from cancer since 1923 and went through another of many surgeries in early 1931. It's doubtful that he was taking new patients.

But if Howard T.'s account is true, Rowland's failure to see Freud was dramatic evidence of further synchronicity at work. Freud had little use for religious conversions and even considered them neurotic. His Austrian colleague Alfred Adler, who was then still practicing in Vienna before emigrating to the United States, also had little confidence in a conversion experience. Adler, who eventually broke away from Freud with an even more ego-centered and rationalistic model of human behavior, probably wouldn't have offered religion as a means of recovery for a suffering alcoholic.

Thus, of the three giants of modern psychoanalytic theory, only Jung acknowledged and actively worked for a deeper understanding of humankind's spiritual nature, and his writings abound with his thoughts on the subject. This was, in fact, one of the subjects that had helped bring about his estrangement from Freud in 1913 following a close friendship that had begun six years earlier with Jung as Freud's devoted disciple.

Jung also deplored the practice of uncovering deep emotional problems without offering the patient much more than his own bootstrap efforts in overcoming them. In a book published in 1933, Jung could have been speaking of the plight of alcoholics when he wrote: "It is well known that Freudian psychoanalysis is limited to the task of making conscious the shadow-side and the evil within us. It simply brings into action the civil war that was latent, and lets it go at that. The patient must deal with it as best he can. Freud has unfortunately overlooked the fact that man has never yet been able singlehanded to hold his own against the powers of darkness—that is, of the unconscious. Man has always stood in need of the spiritual help which each individual's own religion held out to him."[5]

While Jung couldn't have known about them he likely would have agreed that synchronicity was at work in 1931, when the series of "coincidences" that would flower into AA were set into motion. That year, for example, a troubled alcoholic named Russell "Bud" Firestone, second son of the great tire-making pioneer, knelt in prayer in a train compartment with Dr. Sam Shoemaker while returning from a religious convention in Denver. This brought Firestone a dramatic return to sobriety that would have far-reaching influence in Akron, Ohio. In New York, the study of alcoholism as a disease was under way by

15

a few professionals, including Dr. William D. Silkworth, whose contribution would eventually prove invaluable to AA. And professional knowledge of alcoholism as a disease was strengthened in 1931 with the publication of Richard Peabody's *The Common Sense of Drinking*. Peabody's insights in that book, including his statement, "Half measures are to no avail," must have influenced Bill Wilson seven years later in writing perhaps the most turned-to chapter in the Big Book: Chapter Five, "How It Works," where the Twelve Steps are first stated in full.

Rowland H., as the first alcoholic in the relay process that took spiritual truths to Bill Wilson, had a crucial role. It's something of a loss in AA history that Rowland never became an AA member or lent his considerable talents to the early founding of the fellowship. A Yale graduate and a man of great intelligence and ability, he was a director of major corporations and served as a vestryman at Sam Shoemaker's Calvary Church in New York City. Rowland was a member of a prominent Rhode Island family that traces its lineage in America back to 1635. Among his forebears and related to them were industrial pioneers, scholars, and naval heroes. A direct ancestor was a distinguished writer and philosopher and an aunt was president of Wellesley College.

While there's little available information about the two trips Rowland took to consult with Jung in Switzerland, it's likely that the first came in 1931, as Bill believed. Rowland's only surviving son, Charles, remembers that his parents had divorced in 1929 and remarried later. But Charles was too young to remember the part alcoholism must have played in the divorce or if recovery also brought about the reconciliation. He did recall traveling to Europe, probably on the magnificent liner *Ile de France*, in 1931 and staying in France with his brothers and sister while their parents went to Switzerland.

Bill Wilson's belief that Rowland's first consultations with Jung continued for a year has to be qualified, however, by what is known about Jung's methods of dealing with his patients. Rowland and his wife may have lived in or near Zurich while he saw Jung periodically at the doctor's lakeside home in Kusnacht. Writing about Jung for *Harper's* magazine in May 1931, Elizabeth Shepley Sergeant noted that "Doctor Jung's patients must take a little steamboat at a landing haunted by gulls and wild ducks, and then walk a good ten minutes to a yellow country house standing well within walls and gardens on the edge of the Zurichsee."

The patient was greeted by a pack of skirmishing dogs, Sergeant noted, and then escorted to an upstairs study and given tea. While the patient discussed his problems, "Jung tramped the floor, fed the fire, lighted a meditative pipe." Though he could momentarily turn into a German professor, the actual Jung, Sergeant reported, was "solid and vital in his middle fifties," a humorous and skeptical man who refused to stand on a pedestal or to take on any white-bearded Old Testament air. "Yes," he agrees with a young lady, "all men are liars, certainly. I just let them sit in that chair and lie until they get tired of lying. Then they begin to tell the truth." "One leaves Jung's presence," Sergeant added, "feeling enriched and appeased, as by contact with a pine tree in the forest—a life as much below ground as above."

This was the man of great depth whom Rowland H. consulted in what was probably that same study, seeking to unravel the mystery of the alcoholic obsession that was destroying him. Rowland apparently found great support and understanding from Jung, and even believed—as many alcoholics do—that this new knowledge and self-understanding were the answer. Rowland's "admiration for you was boundless," Bill Wilson reminded Jung in the 1961 letter, "and he left you with a feeling of much confidence.

"To his great consternation, he soon relapsed into intoxication," Bill had continued in his letter to Jung. "Certain that you were his 'court of last resort,' he again returned to your care. Then followed the conversation between you that was to become the first link in the chain of events that led to the founding of Alcoholics Anonymous."[6]

Aside from counseling Rowland H., however, Jung had no further role in the development of AA. Bill Wilson did consult his writings and sometimes referred to Jung's belief that people tend to become neurotic around age thirty-five if they have no hope of a future life after death. But Bill made these observations long after AA was well established and on its way to becoming a worldwide fellowship.

In view of the briefness of this encounter, did Jung really deserve the gratitude Bill Wilson expressed toward him? It was Jung's indirect role in AA's founding that brought recent comments from T. Willard Hunter, a longtime Oxford Group member who had been associated with that fellowship since 1936. "All Jung did was tell Rowland that he needed spiritual help," Hunter points out. "The actual electricity he needed for recovery was supplied by the Oxford Group, which was founded by Frank Buchman. Yet AA never gave Buchman any of the credit it extends to Jung."[7]

Thanks partly to Hunter's efforts, AA has been making more acknowledgment of Buchman's role, and the Oxford Group founder's photo was included in the Bill Wilson biography, *Pass It On*, released by AA World Services in 1984.

But Jung's contribution to AA's founding shouldn't be slighted. Though indirect, Jung's work presented a spirit and a philosophy that has partly been embraced by AA. Far from being a casual bystander in the spiritual arena, Jung was a devoted partisan who believed without a doubt that religious experiences produce a power that humans need for overcoming problems and also for achieving their greatest fulfillment. And while he apparently had no *active* part in outlining where and how Rowland H. could find his redemptive conversion experience, Jung's endorsement of the idea certainly gave it credibility. As his letter to Wilson explained, such a recommendation brought certain professional risks. It was not quite respectable, even for a man of Jung's stature, to suggest that a person's only hope lay in religious transformation.

It's still not clear whether Rowland H. made his first connection with the Oxford Group in Europe or somehow found it after returning to the United States. There's a strong case for believing it may have started in Switzerland, since the Oxford Group was already very active there. It's just as plausible that he could have found the Oxford Group in New York City, where Dr. Sam Shoemaker's Calvary Church was virtually the U.S. headquarters of the movement.

Whatever his initial contacts with the Oxford Group might have been, Rowland had found sobriety by early 1934, perhaps with help from Dr. Shoemaker. According to a 1954 interview with Cebra G., one of the alcoholics who assisted him in sponsoring Ebby, Rowland was driving in Massachusetts from South Williamstown to Pittsfield when he heard an inner voice say, "You will never take a drink again." He then threw his pint bottle, a constant companion, into the bushes along the road, according to the account Cebra remembered.[8]

The 1934 date also coincides with the information in a letter written by Rowland to a Denver man in 1937. "My contact with [the Oxford Group] began three years ago," Rowland wrote. "Through their instrumentality, I began to find the answer to conflict and frustration in my own life, and so began to find a new peace, direction and power." He went on to say that his personal experience had convinced him "that in proportion as each one of us lets God take control of his life, we begin to be shown His will and begin to be a part of His plan for the world."[9]

According to several accounts, Rowland was one of the most dedicated Oxford Groupers in New York, Vermont, and upper Massachusetts. Bob Scott, a nonalcoholic who joined the Oxford Group in Williamstown, Massachusetts, in 1936, met Rowland at his first meeting there.[10] This was just south of Shaftsbury, Vermont, where Rowland had a summer home and also operated a real estate office for several years.

Rowland was living in Shaftsbury in 1934 when he began working with Edwin T., the "Ebby" who then became the second torch bearer of what was to evolve into the AA message.

Like Rowland, Ebby was a member of a prominent family whose roots went back to colonial America. His grandfather, uncle, and brother had served with distinction as mayors of Albany, New York, where his father had been an important manufacturer. The family summered in Manchester, Vermont, just north of Shaftsbury, and during his early years Ebby had come to know Bill Wilson, whom he remembered as an outstanding baseball player.

In later years Ebby and Bill had become occasional drinking companions, and on one infamous occasion in 1929 had chartered an airplane to fly from Albany, New York, to Manchester for the opening of a new airport. Arriving drunk, they had disgraced themselves. Later that year, Bill had been bankrupted in the October collapse of the stock market, and for the next five years had drifted deeper into alcoholism, financially supported by his wife. The money in Ebby's family had also run out. He had spent the intervening years in worsening trouble and near-destitution, with the likelihood of being institutionalized, until Rowland H. had intervened.

Ebby, in the summer of 1934, had been living in the Manchester area for two years, periodically getting drunk and into further trouble. At the time that he met Rowland H., Cebra G., and Shep C., there was a likelihood that his latest drunken escapade would fetch him a six-month stay in Vermont's Windsor Prison. But when Rowland H. appeared in court and accepted responsibility for Ebby, the judge, who was Cebra's father, released him to Rowland's custody. Rowland also invited Ebby to live temporarily at his home in Shaftsbury, and then later took him to New York City.

In 1954, Ebby recorded his recollections of Rowland, who had died in 1945. Though the AA system of "sponsorship" and "carrying the message" had yet to be developed with its emphasis on alcoholism, Rowland was practicing it as an Oxford Grouper, particularly in the areas of helping others and seeking guidance through quiet times. Remembering Rowland as "a good guy," Ebby told how his benefactor had come to see him at the old family vacation home in Manchester where Ebby was then living. "The first day he came to see me, he helped me clean up the place," Ebby remembered. "Things were a mess and he helped me straighten it up and he stuck by me from beginning to end. In fact, one time he and I took a trip down through Texas and New Mexico and spent a couple of weeks on a ranch that he owned."

Ebby also recalled Rowland's telling him about his consultations with Carl Jung and how this had given him an understanding of the real difficulties faced by an alcoholic. "During my subsequent traveling around the New England states with him, Rowland gave me a great many things that were of a great value to me later on," Ebby said. "He had had a thorough indoctrination [of Oxford Group principles] and he passed as much of this on to me as he could. When we took trips together, we would get up early in the morning and before we even had any coffee, we would sit down and try to rid ourselves of any thoughts of the material world and see if we couldn't find out the best plan for our lives for that day and to follow whatever guidance came to us.

"I am grateful for all that Rowland did for me," Ebby added. "He impressed upon me the four principles of the Oxford Group, which were Absolute Honesty, Absolute Purity, Absolute Unselfishness, Absolute Love. He was particularly strong in advocating the Absolute Honesty—honesty with yourself, honesty with your fellow man, honesty with God, and these things he followed himself and thereby, by example, he made me believe in them again as I had as a young man."

Rowland's sponsorship was effective in helping Ebby establish what turned out to be a two-year period of sobriety. In the fall, Rowland and Ebby went to New York City. Ebby, after staying for a time with Shep C., went to live at Calvary Mission near First Avenue in lower Manhattan. "It was while I was staying there and working with the Oxford Group that I heard of Bill's difficulty due to drinking," Ebby remembered. "I phoned one day and got Lois, his wife, on the phone and she invited me over to dinner a night or two later. I did, and of course, [that story] is recorded in the Big Book, *Alcoholics Anonymous*. While I was talking to Bill that evening, naturally he was impressed by the fact that I was sober and when I told him the reasons coming from the teachings of the Oxford Group, he, too, was impressed."[11]

Bill Wilson's recollection of their meeting appears in Chapter One, "Bill's Story," in the AA text *Alcoholics Anonymous*. In AA, it is looked upon as a beginning of the process that enabled Bill to get sober and then to carry the message six months later to Dr. Bob Smith in Akron, Ohio, following the collapse of a business venture. The Big Book account clearly shows that Ebby, at that point in his life, was practicing the same essentials of sponsorship that had been passed on to him by Rowland H. and the Oxford Group.

When Ebby called on him, Bill was in the midst of a morbid drinking bout following failed attempts to achieve sobriety at New York's Towns Hospital under the guidance of Dr. William D. Silkworth. Bill was astonished to find Ebby both sober and showing a new confidence and happiness. And it was almost unbelievable that Ebby had no interest in drinking and had been sober for more than two months.

Ebby carefully told Bill what had happened to him. As explained in Bill Wilson's biography, Ebby especially emphasized the idea that he had been hopeless. "He told me how he had got honest about himself and his defects, how he'd been making restitution where it was owed, how he'd tried to practice a brand of giving that demanded no return for himself," Bill recalled in 1954. "Then, very dangerously, he touched upon the subject of prayer and God. He frankly said he expected me to balk at these notions." But as Ebby explained it, this new God-consciousness had released him from his desire for drink and had given him peace of mind and happiness of a kind he had not known for years.[12]

Bill continued to drink after Ebby's visit. But as early AA members were to say later, "the seed had been planted." He could not get the thought of Ebby and his sobriety out of his mind. Ebby called on him again, this time accompanied by Shep C., whom Bill had known for years and did not consider much of a problem drinker. Later on, Bill turned up at Calvary Mission in a drunken, maudlin condition and made a show of giving testimony with other penitents at the altar. Finally, he went back to Towns Hospital and checked in for the last time with the kindly Dr. Silkworth.

Ebby visited Bill again at Towns, and again they discussed the spiritual principles that had enabled Ebby to find sobriety. But Bill was in despair and rebellion, with great doubts about his own ability to recover in the same way. "He wanted the sobriety Ebby had found," his biography reports, "but he couldn't believe in the God Ebby had talked about."

After Ebby left, Bill fell into a deep depression—a state of desperation that he later came to see as the "deflation at depth" that most alcoholics need to recover. "With neither faith nor hope," his biography states, "he cried, 'If there be a God, let him show Himself.' "[13]

This was followed by an incredible experience that has become enshrined in AA as "Bill Wilson's Hot Flash" (see Chapter Five). Bill, in his 1961 letter to Jung, described the experience as "an illumination of enormous impact and dimension." It was an extreme example of an experience that is sometimes called "conversion" and in the Oxford Group was usually called "change." What essentially happened was that in a few seconds Bill underwent a complete transformation in his thoughts and feelings. He was changed from a doubter to a person who *knew*, with absolute certainty, that God existed and was expressed in human life as a Universal, Loving Force. And the change was so complete that both his wife and Dr. Silkworth immediately realized that some great adjustment had taken place in Bill's life.

At the same time that he had this feeling of great power and release, however, Bill also was assailed by doubts as to his sanity. He summoned Dr. Silkworth and described his experience. Dr. Silkworth listened patiently, and then told Bill, "You have been the subject of some great psychic occurrence, something that I don't understand. I've read of these things in books, but I've never seen one myself before. You have had some kind of conversion experience." Whatever the experience, he said, "You are already a different individual. So, my boy, whatever you've got now, you'd better hold on to. It's so much better than what had you only a couple of hours ago."[14]

This helped convince Bill he hadn't merely been the victim of hallucination. Then Ebby arrived with a copy of William James's *The Varieties of Religious Experience*. Ebby reportedly had not read the book, but it had been recommended by Oxford Group members.

In his 1961 letter to Jung, Bill had also commented on the key role of James's book in validating his spiritual experience: "This book gave me the realization that most conversion experiences, whatever their variety, do have a common denominator of ego collapse at depth. The individual faces an impossible dilemma. In my case, the dilemma had been created by my compulsive drinking and the deep feeling of hopelessness had been vastly deepened by my doctor. It was deepened still more by my alcoholic friend when he acquainted me with your verdict of hopelessness respecting Rowland H."[15]

Bill's biography also lists the three "common denominators" he discovered in William James's book. One was *calamity;* each individual in the case histories described by James was experiencing total defeat in some problem area. The second denominator was *admission of defeat,* and the third, *an appeal to a Higher Power.*

Though James made little mention of drinking problems in his book, the three denominators actually made their way into AA as the central concepts in the first three of the Twelve Steps. They also appear as the "three pertinent ideas," or ABCs, in the Big Book's Chapter Five, a section read at many AA meetings:

a) That we were alcoholic and could not manage our own lives.
b) That probably no human power could have relieved our alcoholism.
c) That God could and would if He were sought.[16]

Bill also told Jung that in the wake of his spiritual experience, he had the vision of a society of alcoholics, each identifying with and transmitting his experience to the next—chain-style. "If each sufferer were to carry the news of the scientific hopelessness of alcoholism to each new prospect, he might be able to lay every newcomer wide open to a transforming spiritual experience. This concept proved to be the foundation of such success as Alcoholics Anonymous has since achieved." Bill went on to explain to Jung that this had made conversion experiences of nearly every variety reported by James "available on an almost wholesale basis."[17]

As it turned out, Bill Wilson's transforming spiritual experience was a starting point for his sobriety, but was not an instant answer for all his personal problems. He had many setbacks and faced much opposition before he learned how to carry the same message to others. Members of the Oxford Group, who had done so much to help him, soon began to question his belief that he should limit his work to helping other alcoholics. He had difficulty re-establishing himself in business. Problems with depression and self-pity dogged him constantly.

During these early months of his sobriety, Bill Wilson also discovered that returning to his old hospital to talk to other alcoholics worked some sort of magic on his moods of self-pity and despair. It was something that never failed to lift him up, restoring his confidence and sense of well-being. ("You can't keep it unless you give it away!" was an Oxford Group maxim that has also survived in AA.) This practice of working with others had come to him from Rowland H. and Ebby and, as AA history records, it led Bill Wilson to contact Dr. Bob Smith some months later in Akron.

But it took a number of these seemingly random, yet perfectly timed encounters before Bill Wilson and Dr. Bob Smith could get together in 1935. First, there was Rowland H.'s consultation with Jung in 1931, after which he made one abortive attempt to stay sober and then returned to learn from Jung that a religious conversion might be his only hope for recovery. Rowland found this experience in the Oxford Group, and also settled temporarily in Shaftsbury, Vermont, not far from where Ebby T. was then living. Ebby's escapades brought him into conflict with the law and to the attention of Rowland, who joined Cebra G. and Shep C. in helping him. Rowland took Ebby to New York City, where he found refuge at a mission run by Calvary Church. Ebby then telephoned Bill Wilson at the very time the future AA co-founder was facing complete collapse. Bill then had a transforming spiritual experience that was validated and supported by William James's book. He also learned that helping others is the best way of helping oneself. This soon set in motion another chain of events that took the same program to Dr. Bob Smith in Akron, Ohio.

It wasn't until some years later that Carl Jung coined the term *synchronicity* to describe such perfectly timed but causally unrelated actions. AA members who review the society's origins call it "a series of coincidences" and are then likely to add, "But you and I don't believe in coincidences."

This is their way of saying, of course, that the chance events and ideas that brought AA into being were all guided and directed by a Power greater than any of the people involved.

CHAPTER TWO

What Was the Oxford Group?

In 1978, an enterprising speaker and writer named T. Willard Hunter, then assistant to the president of the School of Theology at Claremont (California), organized a centennial celebration of the birth of Frank N. D. Buchman.

This one hundredth birthday memorial for the Oxford Group founder, who died in 1961, drew cooperation from a number of prominent individuals who had benefited from Buchman's work.

But an invitation to Alcoholics Anonymous—perhaps the greatest beneficiary of all—was politely declined. According to Hunter, he was told by Bob P., then general manager of AA World Services, that there were two problems: (1) the anonymity principle ruled out anyone's speaking for AA; and (2) "I think some of our members," Bob P. added, "would say that we got out of bed with those people—why should we now get back in?"

Bob P. did respond, however, to the idea of an article in the monthly *The AA Grapevine,* with the thought that it would interest readers who had heard repeatedly about AA's origins in the Oxford Group. Here was a timely opportunity to learn more about the Oxford Group's founder.

Hunter's article, though initially encouraged by the magazine's editor and rewritten with the assistance of an AA member, was later rejected with the unanimous approval of the magazine's editorial board. The message in this rejection was that AA wanted no identification with Frank Buchman.

Why has AA, at the public level at least, been so reluctant to acknowledge any tie or debt to a man who helped start the chain of events that eventually launched Alcoholics Anonymous? This is an uncharacteristic stance for a society whose founders, particularly Bill Wilson, wanted to express gratitude to all their benefactors.

There are several likely reasons for that 1978 refusal to become involved with Buchman, even seventeen years after his death. For one thing, Buchman became a controversial person in the late 1930s and was, for a short time, accused of having pro-Hitler sympathies. At the same time, Bill Wilson believed that Buchman and the Oxford Group were getting into trouble with the Roman Catholic church in the late 1930s and, as Wilson put it, "that would have kept a lot of Irishmen from getting sober!"[1] There was also the fact that the Oxford Group, which was called Moral Re-Armament (MRA) after 1938, conveyed the kind of religious and political overtones that AA seeks to avoid. In rejecting involvement with the Buchman centennial, AA World Services executive Bob P. and *The AA Grapevine* editorial board were only being good stewards of AA traditions. Had Bill Wilson been alive in 1978, he might have agreed with the decisions to decline the centennial invitation and reject the magazine article.

Yet, even Wilson conceded that AA's debt to Buchman was enormous. According to AA's official biography of Wilson, he seriously regretted not having personally acknowledged this debt to Buchman. Shortly after Buchman's death in 1961, Bill said in a letter to a friend, "Now that Frank Buchman is gone and I realize more than ever what we owe to him, I wish I had sought him out in recent years to tell him of our appreciation."[2]

Wilson did freely acknowledge AA's debt to the Oxford Group many times, although he did want Jack Alexander to omit any reference to it in the 1941 *Saturday Evening Post* article that became a main spur to the society's growth.[3] One of Wilson's most direct acknowledgments was published by AA in 1957: "[The] early AA got its ideas of self-examination, acknowledgment of character defects, restitution for harm done, and working with others straight from the Oxford Groups and directly from Sam Shoemaker, their former leader in America, and from nowhere else." Wilson had also described the Oxford Group's principles as "ancient and universal ones, the common property of mankind."[4]

This acknowledgment gave due credit to the Oxford Group and focused on Dr. Shoemaker's pivotal role as rector of Calvary Church and eventually as an enthusiastic backer of the fledgling AA movement. What's even more impressive about Shoemaker—as we'll learn in Chapter Four—is that he also had a role in the pre-AA development in Akron, Ohio. Shoemaker was a warm friend and supporter of AA both at Calvary Church in New York City and later on when he served another Episcopal church of the same name in Pittsburgh.

Even though Dr. Shoemaker was most directly responsible for the Oxford Group's influence on AA's founding, he was not the primary founder of the Oxford Group, the instrument of all this activity. Dr. Shoemaker owed his own conversion—which was called "change" in the Oxford Group—to a 1918 meeting in China with Frank Buchman (Chapter Three). And Dr. Shoemaker expressed a personal debt to Buchman even long after breaking with the Oxford Group and its founder in 1941. So what is AA's debt to Frank Buchman if, as Bill Wilson realized, much is owed to him?

Buchman's contributions to AA were both positive and negative—that is, AA learned what to do and what not to do from Buchman's work with the Oxford Group. Much of the "what not to do" is implied in AA's traditions and, in Wilson's opinion, was necessary for AA's survival. This view is widely supported in AA.

On the positive side, AA's debt to Buchman is at least threefold. First, Buchman rediscovered fundamental truths about spiritual change and put them to practical use. He learned that it's necessary to face and release pride and resentment, or any shortcoming or character flaw, in order to find spiritual growth and power. He had a gift for passing this message on to others and helping them find self-understanding and a new spiritual awareness. Using fresh language and catchy terms, Buchman moved the spiritual life out of its stained glass enclosure to where the people are. He coined and borrowed slogans, too, and it's likely that some of AA's slogans, now becoming famous on car bumpers everywhere, came to the fellowship from Frank Buchman.

Buchman also perfected methods of meeting in small groups and sharing experiences in order to practice personal honesty and help others in their growth and change. Finally, and of great importance to AA, he achieved early success in helping alcoholics recover, a process that eventually reached Rowland H. and the people who would start AA.

Offsetting this splendid work, Buchman made some moves that Wilson viewed as highly damaging to the Oxford Group's spiritual mission. One of the most serious problems was a 1936 newspaper account of an interview that made Buchman appear to be pro-Hitler at the very time the Nazi leader was launching the first of his many aggressions. Like the adversarial journalism of more recent years, the newspaper story was a sensational and unfair distortion of Buchman's real position. But it damaged the Group's public image and became one of the reasons Wilson wanted no identification with it later on. It was also an example of the risks of expressing opinions on political issues—something that AA avoids by having no opinions.

Buchman also believed in what came to be called a "key person" strategy that found no place in AA and is, in fact, contrary to AA's democratic ideals. This key person strategy was a process of converting the leading influential people and thereby also drawing in the followers. Though it has some merit, it was considered wrong for AA, whose leaders are supposed to be only trusted servants.

Another problem was that Frank Buchman came to be seen as an authoritarian in spiritual matters. He told his associates to seek spiritual guidance, but sometimes questioned the results. "If the guidance you received didn't agree with his, he'd tell you to go back and seek more guidance!" Willard Hunter concedes.[5] Bill Wilson, though advocating the need for spiritual guidance, became more interested in the idea of listening to the "group conscience."

Bill Wilson also complained about the Oxford Group's aggressive evangelism, insisting that it wouldn't work with alcoholics. Others voiced similar criticisms, and some magazine stories in the early 1930s claimed that Oxford Group meetings could be highly emotional affairs.

Since all of these problems with the Oxford Group would be serious to AA members, it's tempting to say that the fellowship is correct in barely acknowledging any debt to Buchman. It may also be easy to ignore Buchman's contribution since he had no involvement in the actual formation of AA and even considered "helping drunks" to be only one activity in his important mission of changing the world. Why, then, should AA acknowledge any indebtedness to a person who didn't even want such acknowledgment?

Perhaps the best reason, in light of AA principles, is simply to preserve and enhance AA's commitment to its spiritual heritage of truth and honesty. Though AA is built on ancient spiritual principles that are, indeed, the common property of all mankind, most of these ideas came directly to AA through and from the Oxford Group. And the Oxford Group was wholly Frank Buchman's creation. As one longtime Oxford Group member said, to speak of the Oxford Group without discussing Buchman is akin to omitting Henry Ford from an early history of the American automobile industry.

It's even more surprising that many AA members did not know of Buchman's importance to their movement during his later years as the well-publicized leader of Moral Re-Armament. Even knowing this, many of them might have been cool to him, as Wilson reportedly was. Nevertheless, the facts about Buchman deserve to be told for the enlightenment of those interested in AA's spiritual origins. In fact, knowing something about Buchman and his early work is essential in showing the network of relationships that went into the formation of AA.

❧   ❧   ❧

Frank Buchman was born in Pennsburg, Pennsylvania, about fifty miles north of Philadelphia, on June 4, 1878. According to one biographer, he was reared in a warm family environment where "abstinence from alcohol was regarded as preferable, and the only permissible vice was overeating."[6] Though his father eventually operated a saloon in nearby Allentown, Buchman accepted abstinence as a way of life and later believed it was essential in his ability to help problem drinkers.

Even while growing up, Buchman displayed kindly, humanitarian traits and appeared to be primarily interested in helping others. He was a deeply religious youngster, at least in accepting and believing the doctrines of his church. After being trained and ordained as a Lutheran minister, he became director of a Philadelphia hospice for orphan boys in 1905. By all accounts, he performed the work conscientiously and with a great deal of compassion for the disadvantaged youngsters in his care.

But late in 1907, an argument with his trustees over the food budget forced him to resign from the post. When he left America the following January to travel in Europe, he was nursing a swollen, festering resentment toward the six trustees whom he held responsible for the loss of his position. He told his parents that he felt "like a whipped cur, all tired out." His whole heart had been in the hospice, and he had been belittled by men who, he felt, simply did not grasp what he was trying to do.[7]

Carrying his baggage of resentment and self-pity, the thirty-year-old Buchman visited Spain, Egypt, the Holy Land, Greece, Austria, and Germany. Finally arriving in England in July 1908, he decided to attend the famous Keswick Convention of evangelicals, apparently in the hope of meeting F. B. Meyer, a highly acclaimed minister. Desperate and confused,

Buchman was obviously seeking something that might lift him out of his unhappy state.

Meyer was not in Keswick, but the trip, and another minister, changed Buchman's life. The turning point for Buchman came one Sunday afternoon when he wandered into a little Keswick church where a woman evangelist, Jessie Penn-Lewis, was preaching to a small group of about seventeen persons.

In earlier Oxford Group literature, this minister was unidentified. Garth Lean, Buchman's most recent biographer, has given her a name and noted that her husband was a descendant of the family of William Penn.[8] Writer Mark O. Guldseth has traced the more important factor of Mrs. Penn-Lewis's religious lineage, showing that she preached a simple gospel that was directly in the tradition of Dwight L. Moody and Charles Finney (see Chapter Nine).[9]

Jessie Penn-Lewis was no spellbinding orator, but that afternoon she had the power to help Buchman face the pride and bitterness that were destroying him. A. J. Russell noted that "in her simple, straight-forward, conversational talk...[she] spoke about the Cross of Christ, of the sinner and the One who had made full satisfaction for the sins of the world."

Buchman later said that this had been "a doctrine which I knew as a boy, which my church believed, which I had always been taught and which that day became a great reality for me. I had entered the little church with a divided will, nursing pride, selfishness, ill-will, which prevented me from functioning as a Christian minister should. The woman's simple talk personalized the Cross for me that day, and suddenly I had a poignant vision of the Crucified.

"There was infinite suffering on the face of the Master, and I realized for the first time the great abyss separating myself from Him," Buchman later said. "That was all. But it produced in me a vibrant feeling, as though a strong current of life had suddenly been poured into me, and afterwards a dazed sense of a great spiritual shaking-up. There was no longer this feeling of a divided will, no sense of calculation and argument, of oppression and helplessness; a wave of strong emotion, following the will to surrender, rose up within me from the depths of an estranged spiritual life, and seemed to lift my soul from its anchorage of selfishness, bearing it across that great sundering abyss to the foot of the Cross."

Profoundly changed by his realization, Buchman returned to his rooming house and wrote letters of amends to the trustees. Then he shared his experience with another young man during a walk following a conversation at tea. "Before we returned," Buchman said, "he, too, decided to make the surrender of his will to Christ's will. He went to church that night, became a good Christian, and later a successful barrister. And again I had the joy of winning a man to Christ."[10]

Willard Hunter calls the Keswick experience the key to the rest of Buchman's life and work. "It is the recurring type of experience that has launched every major Christian movement since the Apostle Paul," Hunter explains. "Similar turnabouts are recorded in the lives of Francis, Luther, Calvin, Wesley, Booth, Fox, Bunyan, Finney, Moody and others who have provided new directions for broad numbers of individuals and effected widespread social change."

Pointing out that Buchman's conversion had the authentic ring of the intense transitions noted in William James's classic study *The Varieties of Religious Experience,* Hunter also insists that the experience "contains the basic elements of all of Buchman's subsequent work with people, groups, and nations for the next fifty-three years."

Hunter lists these basic elements as (a) an experience of Christ that transforms the individual beyond anything one could possibly do for oneself; (b) prompt restitution for the personal wrongs revealed by the experience; and (c) an immediate chain-reaction, multiplier effect through sharing the experience with others.[11]

In describing his spiritual change, Buchman always used references to the problem of sin and acceptance of Christ that were widely employed in the Oxford Group but never took root in AA. What did take root in AA, however, was the focus on the dangers of resentment and self-pity, and the urgency of releasing these in order to find sobriety, happiness, and well-being. Learning from firsthand experience how resentment had blocked his own spiritual powers, Buchman developed an ability to target the same problem, and additional shortcomings, in the lives of others. With modifications only in style and language, this became the essential method of AA when it began to form as part of the Oxford Group twenty-seven years later.

Returning to the United States following the Keswick experience, Buchman became a YMCA secretary at Pennsylvania State College. Then primarily an agricultural school with fourteen hundred students located in a mid-state rural community, Penn State had little of the academic prestige it enjoys today as a major university. But it gave Buchman the opportunity to work directly with troubled young college men who were seeking new direction in their lives. According to Willard Hunter, Buchman always called this six-year period at Penn State "his laboratory years, working out the principles he was to apply on a global scale."[12]

Several ideas that became useful tools in AA were also perfected by Buchman during his Penn State years. For one thing, he developed the practice of having a "quiet time" to seek divine guidance about any proposed step or action. Though later criticized because of their tendency toward wishful thinking and other pitfalls, quiet times and guidance still have AA advocates.

Buchman also discovered the "key person" strategy at Penn State: "Convert the captain of the football team, and the other students will pay attention." This strategy was to be useful in the early founding of AA, and it was always important to Buchman. But it was essentially contrary to AA's emphasis on anonymity and is discouraged in the fellowship.

One of Buchman's most dramatic Penn State breakthroughs, however, was the conversion of the campus bootlegger, William

Gilliland. Known to students as Bill "Pickle," Gilliland was an alcoholic who then recovered and became a lifelong advocate of Buchman's principles. He was among the first of many problem drinkers who would recover in a Buchman-led movement.

Frank Buchman believed that his own abstinence from alcohol was a vital element in his ability to help change others who had problems. Bill Pickle reportedly said that if Buchman or those working with him had taken even one drop of drink when they first got to know him, he would never have been won to a faith in God that became the helm and sail of his course in life. Frank Buchman put it in these words: "Now I've been reared in circumstances where I could have liquor all my life and whenever I wanted it. But there's one reason why I don't touch a drop. It is because of fellows like Bill Pickle. You don't win them if you touch a drop, just that cocktail. I don't tell anybody else not to drink. Anybody can do anything he wants. Everybody has the liberty of the Spirit, but for my part, I think of men like Bill.

"It's exactly the same with smoking. I don't smoke, but I don't say it's wrong for you. I couldn't do it, because Bill in the old days was a regular chain-smoker. When he changed, everything just dropped off. No smoking, no drinking, although I never said anything to him about it. It is amazing how these—I won't call them sins, I just call them nice little vices—can sometimes be the key to a man's whole life."[13]

The Oxford Group itself was not militantly anti-alcohol, as many religious organizations were. But many of its members apparently gave up both alcohol and cigarettes as part of their "change." Richmond Walker, author of the famous *Twenty-Four Hours a Day* meditation book, reported that he also stopped smoking during the two and one-half years he stayed sober as an Oxford Group member from 1939 to 1941. (He then had an eighteen-month relapse and eventually found his sobriety in the early AA movement in Boston.)[14]

Even Walker's Oxford Group experience brought benefits to AA members, because he incorporated the spiritual ideas of

an Oxford Group book, *God Calling*, in his popular meditation book, which is one of the most widely used publications
among recovering alcoholics.

Jim Newton, an early Oxford Group member whose work
would have an influence on the formation of AA in Akron,
also said that the Oxford Group believed that an alcoholic who
did not stop smoking also would probably return to drinking
at some point.[15]

This emphasis on giving up alcohol as part of "change" apparently helped make the Oxford Group an effective society
in helping alcoholics. Unlike AA, however, the Group did not
seem to possess a body of information about the critical difference between social drinking and alcoholism. Rowland H.,
for example, was an alcoholic who established a firm bond with
Ebby T. and could easily identify with his helpless condition.
But it's doubtful that Shep C., one of the other Oxford
Groupers who assisted Ebby, even had a drinking problem.
He was abstaining from alcohol during the time he worked
with Ebby, but even Bill Wilson, who had known Shep in Manchester, thought he knew little about a real drinking problem.
Shep C. went on to become a colonel during World War II and
later had a highly successful business career as a top officer
in a major corporation. He indicated to an AA member who
interviewed him by telephone in 1980 that he later "drank occasionally" without difficulties.[16]

Following great success with the students at Penn State,
Buchman later became affiliated with Hartford Seminary. The
Hartford assignment was less satisfactory than his work at Penn
State, however, but this may have been partly due to his growing desire to launch what proved to be the missionary phase
of his life's work. Buchman loved to travel, and he was a world
traveler during the 1920s and 1930s when he established the
Group program and built up its strong following. It was called
the First Century Christian Fellowship at one time, and between
1928 and 1938 was known as the Oxford Group.

Even in the 1920s, Buchman was becoming nationally known

and his movement—sometimes called "Buchmanism"—came in for both praise and attacks. It's not surprising that controversy still lingers on about Buchman, because he had a way of drawing criticism even in the early days of his work. At the same time, however, he also attracted a band of fiercely devoted followers who carried on his work with amazing zeal and commitment. This evangelistic fervor, a belief that God was actually guiding them and bestowing them with power, also made the Oxford Groupers so effective in helping a number of alcoholics who became the founding members of AA.

One of the Group's methods was the "house party," a gathering that took place for two, three, or even ten days, often in a resort hotel or a large home loaned by a generous supporter. This idea of a "house-party religion" was extremely new when it was discussed in *Outlook* magazine's January 7, 1925, issue. The writer noted that the purpose of a house party was "to get people to think along right lines, to lead a constructive rather than an aimless and selfish existence, and achieve victory over one's self, to get contact with God, to help America and help the world."

Henrietta Seiberling, the Akron woman who brought Bill Wilson and Dr. Bob Smith together in 1935, defined house parties simply as social gatherings at large places. This could, of course, include residences or hotels. But the Oxford Group also had "small-group" and "large-group" meetings. The small-group meetings, much like AA discussion sessions, were for sharing, with everybody getting to know each other, she said. The large groups were for "witnessing," with people standing up and giving an explanation about how they were changed. These were the forerunners of what came to be called "pitches" or "leads" at open AA meetings.

Oxford Group house parties, like AA meetings, were designed to help win over newcomers while strengthening the faith of others in the group. Though outsiders sometimes wrote disapprovingly of the Oxford Group house parties, the persons who had been changed were convinced that they had found a new direction and purpose in their lives. And they showed evangelistic zeal in working to change others.

One frequent charge made against the Group is that converts sometimes openly discussed their difficulties with sexual problems, still a taboo subject for mixed gatherings in the 1920s. This probably came directly from Buchman's early discovery that many of the young people seeking his help were troubled by conflicts in this area. But none of the critics accused the Group of being permissive or irresponsible in sexual matters, and it now appears that the honesty on this subject was an embarrassment largely to outsiders. In fact, as is common in AA today, the Oxford Group had a practice of assigning men to work with men and women to assist women. But openness in discussing sexual problems did, however, get Buchman's movement expelled from the Princeton campus in the 1920s.

In 1923, the early work of the fellowship was the subject of an excellent book by Harold Begbie titled *More Twice-Born Men*.[17] Begbie, who had completed a definitive two-volume biography of The Salvation Army's General William Booth three years earlier, was a tireless student of religious trends that could be helpful to desperate seekers. His 1909 book, *Twice-Born Men*, had shown how a number of alcoholics recovered in London as a result of undergoing conversion experiences in The Salvation Army (see Chapter Nine). Dedicated to William James, this earlier book about spiritual regeneration certainly had the effect of offering proof that religious experience can be effective in overcoming alcoholism.

In the early 1920s, both Buchman and the fellowship were practicing an anonymity that would soon be abandoned. Begbie, referring to Buchman only as F.B., at his request, identified him as a person whose work was bringing profound changes among the undergraduates of many universities. "He considers privacy essential to his method," Begbie wrote, and added that F.B. "regards publicity as a grave danger. . .and never for one moment dreams of calculating his gains in statistics."

In his preface, Begbie also noted what many would say about

Buchman in later years: that many of his converts disliked his pet phrases and opinions, and yet had an "unconquerable loyalty" to him as "the man who had worked a great miracle in their lives." They thought of him as "by far the most remarkable man of their experience in spite of everything that troubled either their taste or their judgement."

Begbie noted, too, that Buchman's method had "a single characteristic, which struck me at once as going to the very heart and soul of all religious difficulties." This method was to brush aside all the intellectual excuses and to target *sin* as the thing that was locking the door on the distressed spirit's natural peace, natural happiness, and natural power. Begbie also believed that Buchman could see in men's faces an indication of their secret sins, and this gave him an ability to focus almost immediately on what might be troubling another person.

Using personal accounts of persons whom Buchman had changed, Begbie showed how individuals were being transformed by his methods. In one account, Buchman encountered two drunken men on the street and helped one home. "Next day, in the midst of a meeting, F.B. had an irresistible impulsion to go out into the street; someone there wanted him. He left the meeting, went out into the street, and there was the drunken man of last night. F.B. put that man on the right road."[18]

AA members, reading such an account in the enlightened climate of the 1990s, might want to know if the drunken man was really an alcoholic and if he managed to achieve anything approaching permanent sobriety. The significance of such work by Buchman, however, is that he had supreme confidence that his method could help change anybody. This was at a time when many people considered alcoholics hopeless or thought they were lost in sin.

This account was also an example of Buchman's willingness to "follow guidance" on an almost moment-by-moment basis, if necessary. He never lost confidence in his guidance, though it appeared to cause him occasional trouble in subsequent years.

Did Buchman consider alcoholism a sin? If he did, it was apparently with far more tolerance and understanding than many religious reformers seemed to convey. And when the pioneering AA members finally broke with the Oxford Group, it was not because of any tendency to disapprove of alcoholics. The split, when it came, occurred because the groups around Bill Wilson were worried about the Oxford Group's deteriorating public image and also wanted to focus on helping alcoholics.

At various times in later years, there were efforts to show that the Oxford Group had a list of steps or points somewhat similar to the Twelve Steps of Alcoholics Anonymous. There was no such formal program, although there was considerable emphasis on the Four Absolutes: Love, Purity, Unselfishness, and Honesty. These had been developed by Robert Speer and came to Buchman from Professor Henry Wright of Yale University (see Chapter Nine). The Group did have some critical points that were emphasized. Writing in *The Atlantic Monthly* in August 1934, a noted theologian, Henry P. Van Dusen, referred to six points that summarized the Group's work:

1. Men are sinners.
2. Men can be changed.
3. Confession is prerequisite to change.
4. The changed soul has direct access to God.
5. The Age of Miracles has returned.
6. Those who have been changed must change others.[19]

These six points, although not mentioning alcohol, were surprisingly similar to the word-of-mouth program that was developed by Bill Wilson and his friends in the years immediately preceding publication of the book *Alcoholics Anonymous* with its Twelve Step program. According to Bill, the six steps that had come from the Oxford Group were approximately as follows at the top of the next page.

1. We admitted that we were licked, that we were powerless over alcohol.
2. We made a moral inventory of our defects or sins.
3. We confessed or shared our shortcomings with another person in confidence.
4. We made restitution to all those we had harmed by our drinking.
5. We tried to help other alcoholics, with no thought of reward in money or prestige.
6. We prayed to whatever God we thought there was for power to practice these precepts.[20]

There was also an Oxford Group emphasis on a series of steps that resulted in one's "changed life." Frank Buchman listed them as Confidence, Confession, Conviction, Conversion, and Continuance. John W. Drakeford noted that Buchman alliterated these terms—that is, he used a series of words beginning with the same sound.[21] One of Buchman's gifts was in coining simple expressions and easy-to-remember thoughts that captured the essence of his plan.

Confidence, the first phase, was the Oxford Group's method of winning another person's attention and establishing a common ground. People who had been changed, or converted, discussed their own shortcomings and character defects in a way that moved the prospective convert to accept the possibility of wrongdoing in his or her own life. There was also a need to make amends, or restitution, for any past wrongs. This included confession of wrongs and the conviction that a spiritual path was the better way. Continuance was, of course, persistence in maintaining the Oxford Group program in one's own life, and this also involved actively working to help others change.

Quite soon after the release of Begbie's book, Buchman's movement began to attract more followers and considerable publicity at the same time. His privacy was lost as the term *Buchmanism* took hold in the press. There was a tendency of writers who were voicing criticism to use "Buchmanism" rather than the loftier name, Oxford Group. Some writers even felt that Buchman had no right to associate himself in this manner with Britain's most prestigious university! (The name was first used by the press in South Africa to identify a group from Oxford University that was advancing the work there.)

Typical of the extreme criticisms was an item in the March 18, 1933, issue of *Literary Digest,* a prominent weekly journal of the day. Called "'Perils' of Buchmanism," it noted that a Toronto psychiatrist, Dr. G. H. Stevenson, considered the movement a "dangerous delusion" despite the fact that many leading churchmen in North America and England had given it their blessings as a "spiritualizing influence." This criticism warned that Buchmanism had such dangerous features as centering the thought of the individual on sin in his own life, inculcating morbid introspection, discontinuing use of one's intelligence and "substituting a purely emotional subconscious urging which the group regards as guidance from God," inviting mental disorder by insisting that one should listen to "voices," as many of the mentally ill do, and sustained indulgence in emotionalism.

The Christian Century, a journal largely addressed to the Protestant clergy, was also critical of Buchmanism, though primarily because of its emphasis on individual change as the road to social improvements rather than the direct social reform the *Century* editors have consistently advocated.

In the widely circulated publications, however, the Oxford Group received mostly praise. A February 23, 1936, *New York Times Magazine* article called the fellowship a crusade, with a name, "Oxford Groups," that "has become or is fast becoming a household word." Their movement, the subhead stated, held that if the individual could be changed, institutions would also be changed. The Oxford Group was described as a movement that had reached about fifty lands, with a half-dozen of them seriously affected, and "according to all available indications the movement is spreading." Later that year, in its

October issue, *Good Housekeeping* magazine featured a prominent story about a huge June meeting of the Oxford Group
in Stockbridge, a town in the Berkshire Mountains in western
Massachusetts. The huge rally drew ten thousand people
whose international character was emphasized by a display
of flags borne by representatives from many countries (a practice that, whether knowingly borrowed or not, is today part
of the program at AA's international conferences, held every
five years!).

Two of the persons attending this highly acclaimed
Stockbridge meeting were Bill and Lois Wilson. By the following summer, they would withdraw from this remarkable movement that had given them so much in recovery and spiritual
understanding. At about the same time, Bill Wilson would be
launching plans for the preparation of the book that would
become *Alcoholics Anonymous.*

In 1938, Frank Buchman conceived the name Moral Re-
Armament as an answer to the military buildup that was going
on in preparation for World War II. About the same time, the
fellowship began to emphasize larger meetings with prominent persons in attendance. Dropping the Oxford Group name
virtually coincided with the change to MRA and the world-
changing theme. It also coincided with the movement's general
abandonment of the small-group idea that had been so useful
to the formation of AA. In 1939, the alcoholics in Akron, Ohio,
also withdrew from the movement, making complete the earlier
break instigated by Bill Wilson.

Frank Buchman reportedly had an interest in alcoholics'
recovery, but considered it subordinate to the larger task of
finding world peace, an aim that preoccupied him in the remaining years of his life. Willard Hunter quotes Buchman as
saying, "I'm all for helping drunks, but we also have drunken
nations on our hands."[22] Hunter also admits that the Oxford
Group and MRA did not consider helping drunks, at least on
a basis separate from the Group's world-changing mission, as
a "maximum" activity. ("It's not maximum" was the Oxford

Group way of saying that something was not of leading importance. Another Group saying expressing the same idea was, "The good is the enemy of the best.") The movement continues today as Moral Re-Armament, with headquarters in Caux, Switzerland, although its membership and support declined after Buchman's death in 1961.

For Bill Wilson, explaining the early tie to the Oxford Group became a continuing conflict between his concern for honesty and his fear of controversy and public disapproval. He had known Frank Buchman "only to shake hands," but there's no doubt that he considered the Oxford Group founder to be a "loose cannon" in the arena of public relations. Lois Wilson also admitted privately that Bill did not particularly like Buchman.

It's not known if this was why Bill never sought Buchman out to acknowledge AA's debt to him. But perhaps AA's General Service Conference will remedy this oversight one day by releasing some form of acknowledgment.

Alcoholics Anonymous, in its pioneering time, received generous assistance, guidance, and support from many institutions and individuals. Probably no gift surpassed the principles and practices of the Oxford Group, which was a major source for the material of AA's Twelve Steps. Everyone in Twelve Step programs owes a debt of gratitude to Frank Buchman for his singular efforts in laying the foundation for this in the Oxford Group. Buchman was neither an alcoholic nor a close AA supporter in his lifetime, but his work—albeit for the larger world-changing purpose that guided him—had the effect of passing on to the fellowship some of the basic principles of recovery.

CHAPTER THREE

Dr. Sam

In 1918, a twenty-four-year-old Princeton University graduate named Samuel Moor Shoemaker was in Peking (now Beijing), China, teaching business courses sponsored by Princeton. Though Shoemaker knew little about business, the courses were so basic that he was able to cram daily in order to stay ahead of his students.

Such assignments came easily for Shoemaker. He was bright, handsome, and articulate. He got along well with his young Chinese friends, just as he had always fitted in while growing up in affluent circumstances near Baltimore and attending St. George's, an exclusive boarding high school in Newport, Rhode Island. Later on he became a student leader at Princeton.

Despite his exceptional personal qualities, Shoemaker felt that he was failing in one very important area of his life. He had launched a Bible class for the Chinese boys, and attendance was falling off. In three meetings, attendance had declined from twenty to only seven, and he thought something must be wrong with his approach.

While Shoemaker was brooding about this problem, he went to hear a talk by Frank Buchman, who was visiting Peking and addressing various groups. Buchman seemed to have the power to inspire people that Shoemaker felt he lacked. So he made an appointment in hopes of getting Buchman to visit his Bible class.

They met across town from where Shoemaker was living.

The young teacher told Buchman about his background in Maryland, his devotion to the Episcopal church, and the many favorable influences that had pointed him toward the ministry. "When he got to the Chinese picture," wrote Shoemaker's biographer, Irving Harris, "he dwelt on the high qualities of the lads in the Bible class and made bold to suggest that if Buchman could but touch one or two of the leaders of this group, they might well affect the whole student body."[1]

But Buchman did nothing of the sort. While listening to Shoemaker with close, rapt attention that the young Princetonian found flattering, he then asked a personal question: "Tell me, why don't you get through to at least *one* of these fellows—yourself?"

This wasn't the answer Shoemaker wanted to hear—he had always received compliments and other good strokes from religious leaders. Somewhat defensively, he said to Buchman, "If you know the trouble, why not tell me what it is?"

"Might be sin," Buchman replied. Then, according to Harris, Buchman went on to describe how resentment in his own life had, for over a year, kept him from spiritual power and freedom. This had led, of course, to the dramatic Keswick spiritual experience that Frank Buchman shared repeatedly as the great turning point in his own life.

But Shoemaker had not consulted Buchman in order to be told that his own sin might be blocking his power to reach others. Deeply offended, he quickly broke off the discussion and left for his lodgings across town. He rehashed the discussion and thought about his own plans for the future. He also must have felt a deep resentment building up toward Buchman.

But late in the evening, Shoemaker came to another realization that marked the beginning of his spiritual rebirth. "Unable to sleep and strangely moved, he finally slipped to his knees and entered into a wholly fresh spiritual transaction," Harris wrote. Shoemaker now realized how greatly he needed forgiveness, Harris explained. "It seemed to him that he heard someone saying, 'You want to do My work, but in your own way.' As the sense of God's love enfolded him, he agreed that he would serve Him anywhere indefinitely."

Helen Smith Shoemaker, in her biography of her husband, provides Sam's account of his immediate actions following this experience: "Next morning I wakened with an uneasy sense that I must go and talk to my young Chinese business friend, Mr. W. . . . Crossing his threshold, I prayed God to tell me what to say. And it seemed to come to me, 'Tell him what happened to you last night.' My Chinese friend asked me to sit down, and in a pair of creaky wicker chairs we began to talk. 'I believe you have been interested in my class,' I began, 'but not satisfied with it. The fault has been mine. May I tell you something that happened to me last night?' He listened to my story intently and when I had finished surprised me with, 'I wish that could happen to me.' 'It can,' I replied, 'if you will let God in completely.' And that day he made his decision and found Christ. The person God uses is always blessed as well as the one with whom he is used, on the principle that a pipe carrying water gets wet itself on the inside."[2]

His resentment dissolved, Shoemaker also returned to tell Buchman about his dramatic change. This marked the beginning of a rich and exciting friendship for both men. For the next twenty-two years, they would be closely associated in fellowship. Though they would split in 1941, Shoemaker would always acknowledge his great debt to Buchman. He noted this about Buchman's method:

"Frank Buchman knew, as do few spiritual leaders, the value of getting a young convert on his feet to begin witnessing about what has happened to him, and bringing him in contact with other persons on a team in action; and also of keeping in touch with him by letters. He wrote me dozens of them in the ensuing weeks and months. I hooked up again with him whenever he was within striking distance. In those days he sometimes called himself a 'missionary to the missionaries,' and heaven knows most of us needed one."[3]

Both men had been called to the ministerial profession in

mainstream churches, Buchman as a Lutheran and Shoemaker as an Episcopalian. While they were able to form a close association, they were men whose appearance, personalities, and backgrounds contrasted sharply.

Buchman, although six feet tall and usually having a pleasant expression, had none of Shoemaker's commanding presence. Willard Hunter even said that Buchman was a physically unattractive man who believed that God had made him that way for a purpose![4] While Buchman may have exaggerated this, his photographs reveal him as balding and portly, and he was often given an unflattering physical description. When Buchman spoke in Akron in early 1933 (at a rally that would prove to be important to AA's future), an *Akron Beacon Journal* reporter supplied this astonishing portrait: "His face is so sharply cut—a long nose, with close set eyes glittering on each side, a wide straight mouth, and a double chin above a wing collar—that he looks like a charcoal drawing of himself." The reporter, Ruth McKenney, also added that Buchman "does not have a spiritual look, yet he has founded and carried on this religious movement."

Ms. McKenney might have found more to praise in Sam Shoemaker's appearance. He was stockily built and ruggedly handsome, with flashing blue eyes, wavy hair, and a gentle, persuasive manner of speaking. Viewing the two men, a movie casting director would have given Shoemaker the role of a forceful leading man while assigning Buchman a bit part as the worried hotel clerk.

There were also important class differences in their backgrounds. Buchman had grown up in a rural Pennsylvania Dutch community, in decent but hardly affluent circumstances. Shoemaker had lived on his family's country estate in Maryland, accustomed to servants and special privileges, with the expectation of attending a boarding school and Princeton University. He was comfortable and casual with most of the people whose social status and professional attainments always awed Buchman.

But their common bond was the meeting in Peking, where Buchman's challenge had helped engineer a change for Shoemaker that would influence his entire life. Since Shoemaker eventually became a spiritual mentor for Bill Wilson as well as an enthusiastic supporter of AA, it's important to look at this moment of great change for its eventual effect upon AA. Up to this time, Shoemaker had been a highly respectable young man with outstanding personal qualities and an excellent family and educational background. But these advantages were not sufficient for what he really wanted to do in religious work. There still had to be a complete surrender of pride, self-will, and anything else under the heading of "sin." The moment Shoemaker did this, his life changed and he became virtually a new man, a "born-again" person. This also positioned him for the great service that would become so important to Wilson and AA some sixteen years later.

This was the vital secret Shoemaker learned from Frank Buchman. And though the language is different (AA members rarely use the term *sin*, for example), the same message that Buchman conveyed to Shoemaker is essentially what goes on in Alcoholics Anonymous today. The fundamental idea is that pride and resentment, or any kind of self-will, block the flow of spiritual power. People must face such shortcomings in their own lives before they can have anything of real substance to pass on to others.

Shoemaker himself reviewed this basic process at the 1955 International Conference of AA in St. Louis. "I believe there are four universal factors in all genuine spiritual awakenings: conversion, prayer, fellowship, and witness," he told the large assembly. "By conversion I mean the place where a person turns toward God. . . . Prayer, either private or group or public, is the place where we get in touch with God and God's power." He went on to describe fellowship as occurring among people who know they have a great need, while witness was— "by life and by word"—sharing the beginnings of a victory after a spiritual change has aroused the interest of others.[5]

Shoemaker, after his remarkable conversion experience in 1918, became a devoted member of Buchman's group—which soon became known as the First Century Christian Fellowship. Returning to the United States in 1919, he accepted a position at Princeton University. Meanwhile, he attended General and Union Theological seminaries in New York City and was ordained to the Episcopal priesthood in 1921. Only three years later he was called to become rector of Calvary Church in New York City—an extraordinary opportunity for a man of thirty with a relatively short time in the priesthood.

Shoemaker stayed twenty-eight years at Calvary Church before going to Pittsburgh in 1952. Calvary adjoined Gramercy Park in lower Manhattan and had a congregation of well-educated professional and business people, with a sprinkling of older families in New York's upper-class stratum. During Dr. Sam's early ministry there, two projects were completed that had a bearing on the formation of AA. One project was the construction of Calvary House in 1928, which provided space for staff offices and meetings. And as a result of Sam's commitment to the Oxford Group, Calvary House also became that fellowship's U.S. headquarters in the 1930s. Bill and Lois Wilson would be among those attending Oxford Group meetings at Calvary House in 1935 and 1936.

A second Sam Shoemaker project that influenced AA's birth was the establishment of Calvary Mission on East 23rd Street on New York's lower East Side. Originally a chapel, the Calvary Mission structure was vacant and unused when Sam joined Calvary Church. The property was still owned by the church, however, and Shoemaker found a man named Henry Harrison Hadley II to run the mission.

"Harry" Hadley was the son of S. H. Hadley, whose personal testimony of his conversion experience was one of the key examples in William James's *The Varieties of Religious Experience.* Homeless and destitute from alcoholism, S. H. Hadley had undergone a miraculous spiritual change at Jerry McAuley's famous Water Street Mission in New York and then, according to James, "became an active and useful rescuer of drunkards in New York." Describing the result of his conversion experience, Hadley had said, "From that moment till now I have never wanted a drink of whiskey, and I have never seen money enough to make me take one. I promised God that night that if he would take away the appetite for strong drink, I would work for him all my life. He has done his part, and I have been trying to do mine."[6]

Harry Hadley also had personal problems but found a new direction in his life through spiritual change. Before meeting Sam Shoemaker, he had been praying for guidance in finding an opportunity to enter rescue-mission work as his father had. Supported by Calvary Church, the Mission was opened in 1926, providing living space for fifty-seven homeless men and two meals a day for most of them.

Though Calvary Mission was sponsored by an Episcopal church with a sophisticated congregation, its religious meetings were evangelistic and hit hard on the need for sobriety. The mission and its message were much like those at similar havens still operated today by The Salvation Army and other religious organizations. The emphasis was on helping men "change," and it reflected Sam Shoemaker's belief—based on his own experience—that it takes a conversion experience to really transform one's life. And though men with many kinds of problems undoubtedly came to Calvary Mission, a large number of those helped there were certainly alcoholics.

Quoting a parishioner, Helen Smith Shoemaker described the Calvary Mission meeting room as a "clean, bare, yellow place, hard benches, a platform one step up, [with] a huge black cross on the wall." A woman softly played hymns while men drifted in: "They seemed sodden with an exhaustion that was of heart, body and spirit." Then they sang three or four gospel hymns and Mr. Hadley told the story of his own life and conversion. Following this, there might be testimony from men in the audience. One man, for example, got to his feet and said, "I want to give thanks for seven days without drinking."[7]

This Bowery-type rescue mission was only a few blocks east of the upscale Calvary Church neighborhood, and Sam Shoemaker invited its residents and those associated with it to give testimony at Calvary services. It was an unusual but effective blending of the basic Salvation Army kind of message with the more sophisticated Episcopalianism—but it worked. A. J. Russell told about Harry Hadley's bringing more than a hundred men to a Calvary Church service. "Instead of a sermon these men were invited to stand in their pews and tell what contact with Christ had meant to them," Russell wrote. "If ever one was conscious of the Holy Spirit in a church service it was at that extraordinary Evensong.

"There was no waiting. Men popped up one after the other from all points of the front rows of pews and rattled out their life-stories. The pathetic tales they told of broken homes mended, of drunkenness cured, of victory over vice, of the new reign of love in lives and homes previously disordered, divided, discordant, would have melted the heart of the most complacent modern Pharisee," Russell said. He went on to explain how these testimonies then brought responses in the form of an Altar Call, with many of the other church members coming forward and dedicating their lives to God.[8]

Calvary Mission was in operation ten years, finally closing in 1936 after aiding two hundred thousand homeless men who were said to have visited there. Its outstanding resident, for AA's purposes, was Ebby T., who was staying there when he telephoned Bill Wilson in late 1934. Following Ebby's contact with him, Bill Wilson also made an appearance at the Mission during his final drinking bout. Bill's biography describes this visit as well as a maudlin attempt by Bill to join other penitents at the altar![9]

Ebby, during his stay at the Mission, was also diligent in working with other alcoholics and following the Oxford Group program. In reflecting on this historic meeting, it would be hard to exaggerate the importance of the Mission to the linkup with Bill Wilson. Had the Mission not been there, it's doubtful that

Ebby would have remained in New York City following his stay at Shep C.'s apartment. Most likely, he would have returned to Albany where there was at least the hope of some assistance from his brothers.

There's also the fact that Sam Shoemaker and the leadership at Calvary Mission urged their converts to work with others, in the Oxford Group manner. In telephoning Bill, Ebby was not only getting in touch with an old friend; he was also carrying out the Mission's aim and purpose of carrying its message to others who were still suffering.

Calvary House, attached to Calvary Church itself, was the further development in Sam Shoemaker's ministry that became important to the founding of AA. Shoemaker, mainly as a result of his deep involvement in Buchman's movement, permitted the fellowship to meet in Calvary House and establish offices there as U.S. headquarters for the Oxford Group.

Opened in 1928, Calvary House was a seven-story building with a main Great Hall that could seat about two hundred people. It had been built in the late 1920s, largely because Sam Shoemaker believed in small-group activity in connection with the church and insisted that they provide space for these affairs. The building also provided office space, dining facilities, and living quarters for church staff. Additionally, it served as the rectory, since the seventh floor held a duplex apartment where Sam and Helen Shoemaker lived following their marriage in 1930.

"The building was often called a Spiritual Power House," Helen Shoemaker said, "and increasing numbers of visitors from all over the world thought of it in such terms. They came in 1932 and 1933 and throughout the years thereafter from every part of the world . . . many already with a genuine experience of Christ, which had transformed their lives, to learn how to make that experience available to others, and how to relate it intelligently to the needs of the people whom they touched. 'They learned by doing.' " She noted, too, that when "Sam came to Calvary there were no groups whatever of this kind.

He had a vision that there might be some day, but he did not go about creating them by setting up the forms which they eventually were to take. The new life came first, demanding channels for its expression, and the gradual growth and multiplication of these groups provided those channels. The natural order was: change lives first; then provide groups for their fellowship and training so that the message could be spread."[10]

Though all of this group activity went on under the aegis of an Episcopal church, it was really the Oxford Group idea and connection that made it work so well. Jack Smith, who became assistant rector under Sam Shoemaker, was credited with much of the administrative work that made it succeed. (Yet it was Smith who later opposed the idea of a separate group for alcoholics, which Bill Wilson formed following his return from Akron in 1935. And since Smith was such a trusted associate of Shoemaker's, this might explain why Sam apparently did not rally to Bill's defense at this time.)

As an Episcopal clergyman, Shoemaker attracted a large following and was highly respected in church circles as well as by ministers of other denominations. He authored more than twenty books, for example, and was published and quoted in many religious journals. Though he was positioned as a modernist minister with an evangelical approach, he got along well even with people who disagreed with him. Bill Wilson expressed gratitude to Shoemaker many times. In a February 1967 *AA Grapevine* memorial to Sam (who died in 1963), Bill wrote: "Dr. Sam Shoemaker was one of AA's indispensables. Had it not been for his ministry to us in our early time, our Fellowship would not be in existence today." In other writings, Bill also credited Shoemaker with helping him to get a better understanding and acceptance of religion.

Shoemaker, who acknowledged a similar indebtedness to Frank Buchman, finally parted company with the Oxford Group founder in 1941. It was a sad, highly publicized break, and it involved asking Frank Buchman to remove all personal and Oxford Group material and personnel from Calvary House.

Shoemaker's public statement about the parting, recorded in Garth Lean's 1988 book, *On the Tail of a Comet,* explained that certain policies and points of view had arisen in the development of Moral Re-Armament (by then, the new name of the Oxford Group), about which "we have had increasing misgivings."[11] Though these policies and points of view were not described, they were evidently related to MRA's new direction as a more assertive world-changing fellowship with an emphasis on large meetings and attracting influential national leaders. It was also thought that MRA's presence at Calvary Church was beginning to intrude on the regular work of the parish.

The rupture brought deep sorrow to Frank Buchman, Lean wrote. "I have not resigned from Sam," was Buchman's comment, according to Willard Hunter. Buchman was unshakable in his belief that he was being God-guided in the new MRA program, which he promoted with zeal and conviction during the final twenty years of his life. Shoemaker, for his part, launched the Faith At Work movement, which was essentially a new version of the small-group work that had characterized the former Oxford Group. It was fair to say that in the years of AA's rapid growth in the 1940s and 1950s, AA was more in tune with the Faith At Work idea than with the well-publicized MRA movement.

The split also brought a realignment of loyalties, with some longtime Oxford Group members staying with Buchman and others electing to go with Shoemaker. Some of Frank Buchman's associates who stayed in his camp, including Willard Hunter, still felt that Buchman owed Shoemaker an apology for harming him during the final years of their association. They felt Buchman had not listened sufficiently to one of the movement's most effective workers, which Shoemaker certainly was. But Buchman, the man who had done so much to stress the importance of admitting one's wrongs and making restitution, never saw it that way. He did forgive Sam for evicting them from Calvary House, and Shoemaker expressed concern for but not resentment toward Buchman.

Their close friendship, however, was over—a regrettable outcome in view of the help each had given the other.

Shoemaker, in his references to Buchman's movement after the split, always referred to the earlier period (before MRA) as its better days. Writing to Bill Wilson on June 27, 1949, Sam also commended him on his adherence to what AA members call anonymity. "God has saved you from the love of spotlight," Sam wrote to Bill, adding, "at least if not from the love of it—from getting too much into it, and it is one of the biggest things about you. I often speak of it. If dear Frank [Buchman] could have learned the same lesson long ago MRA might have changed the face of the earth."[12]

While Sam Shoemaker was considered for a bishop's post in the Episcopal Church, this never happened, perhaps because his emphasis on individual conversions was considered outmoded by many who wanted the church to be more socially involved. Following his twenty-eight years in New York, he served another Calvary Church in Pittsburgh, where he launched prayer-group movements for young married couples, business people, laborers, and others. His Pittsburgh Experiment for business and labor people continues as one of his most successful ventures and involves executives of the city's leading organizations. In 1955, the same year he addressed AA's Second International Conference, Sam Shoemaker also was named Pittsburgh's Man of the Year in Religion.

Failing health finally forced him to retire in 1962, and he died the following year. At his death, condolences came from religious leaders everywhere, including his good friends Norman Vincent Peale and Billy Graham. Graham, referring to Sam's passing as "the home-going of our beloved Sam," added, "What a blessing it has been for me to talk and especially to pray with this giant among men. I doubt that any man in our generation has made a greater impact for God on the Christian world than did Sam Shoemaker."[13]

Bill Wilson, who went to Maryland for Sam Shoemaker's funeral services, expressed similar gratitude on behalf of AA.

And writing in *The AA Grapevine* in February 1967, Bill stated that Shoemaker "will always be found in our annals as the one whose inspired example and teaching did the most to show us how to create the spiritual climate in which we alcoholics may survive and then proceed to grow. AA owes a debt of timeless gratitude for all that God sent to us through Sam and his friends in the early days of AA's infancy."

CHAPTER FOUR

Setting the Stage in Akron

A few years after AA became airborne, arguments began over where the movement was founded and whether the "best-quality AA" was available in the Midwest or in the New York area.

AA itself answered the first question by acknowledging Akron, Ohio, as the birthplace of AA and formally dating the fellowship's origin as June 10, 1935—the day co-founder Dr. Bob Smith took his last drink.

As for the other question about where the "best-quality AA" is to be found, no fair person would venture a guess. Even today, nobody knows how to account for AA's booming success in certain cities and more lackluster performance in other places.

It is a fact, however, that the alcoholic group in Akron drew in more members in the late 1930s than the companion movement in New York. Bill Wilson was quick to acknowledge this, as he did when pointing out that two-thirds of the Big Book personal stories came from the Akron area. It was also a 1938 report on the Akron movement by Frank Amos that helped convince John D. Rockefeller, Jr., that the fellowship deserved his backing. Later on, Jack Alexander's visit to Akron and Cleveland AA groups helped convince him that he was really onto something for his influential 1941 *Saturday Evening Post* story about AA.

One reason for AA's astonishing early growth in Akron is that Dr. Bob Smith and his wife Anne were gifted sponsors

61

whose personalities and humility helped draw people into the movement. Additionally, it seemed true in early AA groups that medical doctors who recovered from alcoholism became instant authority figures who could impress and move others. There is a possibility, too, that the recovery program received a better reception in a more traditional middle-class, family-oriented community such as Akron than in Manhattan.

But another important, obvious reason for AA's early success in Akron is almost never pointed out. Akron AA got off to a running start because the stage was being set months before Bill Wilson made his fateful business trip out there in 1935. Long before Bill arrived in Akron, a band of Oxford Group members had begun meeting and praying for daily guidance about different problems. Dr. Bob Smith describes them thus in his personal story in the AA Big Book (a recent attempt to limit his drinking to beer had failed):

> About the time of the beer experiment I was thrown in with a crowd of people who attracted me because of their seeming poise, health, and happiness.... I sensed they had something I did not have, from which I might readily profit. I learned that it was something of a spiritual nature, which did not appeal to me very much, but I thought it could do no harm. I gave the matter much time and study for the next two and a half years, but still got tight every night nevertheless.[1]

This reference to the "beer experiment" and "the next two and a half years" place Dr. Bob's first contact with the Oxford Group in 1933. That's when the fellowship was launched in the city with a dramatic Oxford Group rally that dominated local news while it was under way. And any honest discussion of AA's spiritual roots should take this into account.

AA's traditional histories of the now-famous meeting between Bill Wilson and Dr. Bob Smith have always focused on the immediate events that put them in touch with each other in 1935. Bill, then sober about six months, had been in Akron waging a proxy fight for control of a small machine tool company. Losing out in the shareholders' voting, he had found himself pacing the lobby in the Mayflower Hotel, restless and discouraged and not knowing how to spend the weekend.

He feared that he might be tempted to go into the bar to seek companionship. Instead, he called a clergyman, the Reverend Walter Tunks, for the name of an alcoholic he might help. In calling Tunks, Bill found an ardent Oxford Group supporter, but Lois thought he actually chose Tunks only because he liked unusual names. Tunks gave him a list of ten people to call. This led Bill to Henrietta Seiberling, who introduced him to Dr. Bob the following day.

In reviewing this fortunate meeting, however, little attention has been paid to steps that put everything in place. How was it that Henrietta Seiberling happened to be a member of the Oxford Group? What brought the Group to Akron in the first place? Why did Mrs. Seiberling respond so quickly to the idea of introducing Bill to another alcoholic? What had made the Oxford Group such a strong force in Akron compared with other cities? And how did it happen that it was the Akron Oxford Group that was known from the start as a fellowship that could help alcoholics?

The story of the Oxford Group's coming to Akron really started back in 1924, when a young luggage salesman named James D. Newton walked into the "wrong building" at Toy Town Tavern, a winter sports hotel in Winchendon, Massachusetts, where he was staying for the weekend. Newton, eyeing several young women in the room, had expected to attend a dance. Instead, he misunderstood the directions and found himself at a meeting of the fellowship that became known as the Oxford Group a few years later. Before the weekend was over, Newton had been spiritually changed, and the course of his life took a new path.

He found the new course, he always said later, by learning to use the Sermon on the Mount as a guide for his actions and motives. Another young man at the resort explained how this had been reduced to the four absolute standards—honesty, purity, unselfishness, and love.

Back at work in his territory, Newton began to put this guidance into practice by admitting to one of his merchant customers that he'd previously cut corners in dealing with him. But now, he explained, he'd taken a new direction in his life. He also told the man that he'd been reluctant to admit he'd cut corners because he was afraid the merchant would lose respect for him.

But the dealer surprised Newton by saying, "Young man, you've been honest with me, so I'll be honest with you. Till now, I never did have any respect for you."[2]

Newton, a man of great ability, was hired in 1928 to come to Akron as a personal assistant to Harvey Firestone, Sr. Newton was twenty-three years old. Before long, however, he was in charge of the Firestone company's national real estate developments. Newton also became a close friend and confidante of Harvey Firestone's second oldest son, Russell, a likable and idealistic young man whom everybody called Bud.

Bud Firestone seemingly had everything going for him in life—good looks, wealth, a Princeton education, an attractive wife, charm, and considerable business ability of his own (though, like his brothers, he would have undoubtedly felt overshadowed by his famous father).

Bud also had a serious problem. "Bud was a real alcoholic," Newton said, when interviewed at his Fort Myers Beach, Florida, real estate office in 1981. "He consumed as much as two quarts a day on benders and had been in three institutions."[3] Leonard Firestone, Bud's younger brother, objected to this extreme description of Bud's drinking, but conceded that he had difficulties.

Bud's drinking was breaking his parents' hearts. Drying out at expensive institutions helped him get back in shape physically, but he was unable to stay sober.

Newton was convinced that Bud could find his answer in the spiritual program of the Oxford Group. They worked together for months, and even in 1981 Newton recalled the almost superhuman efforts Firestone made in an attempt to whip his problem. "He was trying," Newton said. In hotel rooms on trips, he recalled, they prayed together on their knees: "Bud's tears would wet the side of the bed. He was trying, but there was no victory."[4]

The breakthrough came on a train trip Newton and Firestone took to Denver in 1931. They were going to an Episcopal church conference, but Newton said Oxford Group team members also were with them. On the way out to Denver, Newton persuaded Bud to give him the hip flask he carried. (Such flasks were popular during Prohibition years.) He gave Bud a drink whenever he needed it, but Newton thought that "asking for the flask" would help cut down on the amount consumed.

The talks at the conference deeply impressed Firestone, and on the return trip, Sam Shoemaker joined them. After a time, Shoemaker and Firestone went into a private compartment on the train for a talk.

Something then happened that changed Bud swiftly and dramatically. Newton believed that Bud Firestone was able to share with Sam "the thing that had really defeated him." Perhaps it was something like today's Fifth Step work in AA. "Whatever it was, he finally let go of his own will," Newton said. "He gave his will and his life to God. When he came out of that room with Sam, you could see the difference in Bud's face already."[5]

Harvey Firestone, Sr., was deeply moved and, of course, simply delighted with the change in his son. Out of gratitude, coupled with his own enthusiasm about the Oxford Group, the senior Firestone led others in sponsoring a large weekend Oxford Group conference in Akron in January 1933. It was a major event, headquartered in the Mayflower Hotel but fanning out to churches and other places throughout the city—"even factories," Newton said. An exciting, spectacular affair, it received daily front-page coverage by the *Akron Times-Press* and the *Akron Beacon Journal*.

Frank Buchman, accompanied by twenty-nine members of his team, came to Akron for the affair. A newspaper photograph shows Buchman being met at the Akron railroad station by Dorothy Firestone (Bud's wife) and the Reverend Walter Tunks (the same Walter Tunks whom Bill Wilson would call in May 1935 in his search for an alcoholic).

These huge Akron meetings were markedly different from the small-group idea that had served the Oxford Group so well. And in some ways, they were an indication of the future direction the Group would take as the fellowship evolved into Moral Re-Armament in the late 1930s. For one thing, the Akron conference was an outstanding example of the "key person" strategy at work—changing the leaders so the others will follow. Harvey Firestone, Sr., was such a key person, not only in Akron but nationally. His influence and financial backing were certainly main reasons why the conference attracted so much attention. The newspaper accounts noted, for example, that attendees were some of Akron's most prominent industrialists, such as Paul Litchfield of Goodyear and Frank A. Seiberling, Henrietta's father-in-law and founder of the Goodyear and Seiberling rubber companies.

Another feature of the meetings—and this was important in the formation of AA—was the focus on Bud Firestone's dramatic recovery from alcoholism. This had the effect, Jim Newton said, of positioning the Akron Oxford Group as a society with special expertise in helping drunks. In other areas, the Groups were known for general life-changing work, but in Akron the recovery of Firestone had particularly emphasized the special task of helping alcoholics.

According to Dr. Bob's daughter, Sue Smith Windows, her mother attended the rally meetings, but Dr. Bob didn't. If he was in town during the weekend when the largest meetings were held, however, he would have been aware of the excitement in the area around his downtown office. Another fact of significance is that the rally was almost exactly two and one-half years before Bob's meeting with Bill—coinciding with the account in Dr. Bob's personal story. His attendance at Group meetings apparently started immediately following the rally.

It's likely too that Dr. Bob already knew about Bud Firestone's drinking problem and his sudden recovery sixteen months earlier. Bud, as a member of one of Akron's most distinguished families, may have been the talk of the town when he was drinking. Though the drinking problem was not mentioned in the newspaper accounts, Bud and his grateful wife were fearless in their sharing at the banquet and rally. "I gave my life to Jesus Christ," Firestone told some of the nearly two thousand people in Polsky's auditorium on Friday evening, January 20, 1933. "I let God guide my life now, and I am thankful and full of rejoicing for this Akron meeting."[6]

This event launched the Oxford Group as a regular activity in Akron. And for AA's future and Dr. Bob's eventual recovery, the key people were to be Henrietta Seiberling and T. Henry and Clarace Williams. Like many of today's AA members, they were people who probably wouldn't have been friends without the common bond of their fellowship. Henrietta Seiberling, for example, was at first annoyed when Clarace Williams began pursuing her in friendship. As it turned out, however, this friendship became a step in the founding of AA. And though none had drinking problems, Henrietta and the Williamses had found personal change in the Oxford Group program.

In Henrietta's case, a troubled marriage was taking its toll. She had married John Seiberling, the son of prominent industrialist Frank Seiberling. Though they lived in seeming affluence in Stan Hywet, the fifty-room mansion Seiberling had built in 1917, the family fortunes had ebbed considerably from the days when Mr. Seiberling controlled Goodyear. Unable to patch up her marriage difficulties, Henrietta finally moved, with her three children, to the gatehouse at the entrance to the Stan Hywet grounds. (Never divorced but permanently separated from her husband, Henrietta moved to New York City in 1943, where she lived until her death in 1979.)

The 1933 Oxford Group rally had given Henrietta a new

spiritual anchor in her life, a quality that others noticed. She learned to believe in Divine Guidance, and in the Oxford Group sessions she also began to appreciate people whom she might have ignored earlier.

T. Henry and Clarace Williams, though living in a fine new home at 676 Palisades Drive, were not really in the upper social class with the Seiberling family. They became Henrietta's friends, however, and they joined with her in helping Dr. Bob Smith admit his problem and in praying for his recovery. The Williams home also became the center for the Akron AA group, which moved to King School in 1939 and still claims the honor of being the first AA group in Akron, though now meeting at another location.

While T. Henry never had a drinking problem, his daughter Dorothy recalled that he was deeply concerned about the plight of alcoholics and their families. She remembers riding with her father on a streetcar and seeing drunken, disorderly men being kicked off the car. "It always upset him," she said, "and he'd say, 'What about their poor families?' Drinking particularly upset him. He never drank, but it upset him. So for years, I'm sure he had it in his mind for something he could do for these people."[7]

T. Henry had also undergone personal difficulties that the Oxford Group principles helped him face. Bill D., the first AA member to be sponsored by Bill Wilson and Dr. Bob Smith, said that T. Henry was so despondent about the depression-induced loss of his job and the prospect of losing his house that for a time he simply lay in bed staring at the ceiling. His daughter did not remember such a reaction, but this may have been something the Williamses kept from her and shared only with friends at the Oxford Group meetings.

T. Henry, a native of Connecticut and a direct descendent of Rhode Island founder Roger Williams, was a gifted machine-tool designer. He was chief engineer of National Rubber Machinery, by coincidence the same tool company Bill Wilson was seeking to win in the 1935 proxy fight. T. Henry lost his job in that dispute, and for a time had to work for a small fraction of his former pay. The Williamses were able to retain their beautiful home only because the mortgage-holder was tired of foreclosures and was willing to settle for interest-only payments. According to Bill D., the Williamses also made a spiritual commitment during this low period to give their home for service—hence, the special meetings for alcoholics.[8]

But both Henrietta Seiberling and the Williamses had been dedicated Oxford Group members during the more than two years between the 1933 rally and Bill Wilson's arrival in Akron. Henrietta was especially diligent in calling attention to the Oxford Group work done before Bill came to Akron.

In 1971, the Akron AA groups invited her to the annual Founders Day anniversary to talk about her role in this historic meeting. But she was elderly by this time and did not feel up to the trip from New York City to Akron. A tape recording of her recollections was presented at the anniversary by her son, U.S. Congressman John F. Seiberling. As a youth of fourteen, he had accompanied her to the 1933 Oxford Group meetings and had met Frank Buchman, who gave him a copy of *For Sinners Only*. The following is a portion of the transcription of the tape, setting forth her memories of this earlier time:

Bob and Anne [Smith] came into the Oxford Group, which...was the movement which tried to recapture the power of First Century Christianity in the modern world, and a quality of life which we must always exercise. Someone spoke to me about Dr. Bob's drinking.

He didn't think that people knew it. And I decided that the people who shared in the Oxford Group had never shared very costly things to make Bob lose his pride and share what he thought would cost him a great deal. So I decided to gather together some Oxford Group people for a meeting. That was in T. Henry Williams's house. We met afterwards there for five or six years every Wednesday night.

I warned Anne that I was going to have this meeting. I
didn't tell her it was for Bob, but I said, "Come prepared
to mean business. There is going to be no pussyfooting
around." And we all shared very deeply our shortcomings,
and what we had victory over. And then there was
silence, and I waited and thought, "Will Bob say anything?" Sure enough, in that deep serious tone of his, he
said, "Well, you good people have all shared things that I
am sure were very costly to you, and I am going to tell
you something which may cost me my profession. I am a
silent drinker, and I can't stop."[9] This was weeks before Bill
came to Akron. So we said, "Do you want us to pray for
you?" And he said, "Yes." Then someone said, "Do you
want to go down on your knees and pray?" And he said,
"Yes." So we did.*

And the next morning, I, who knew nothing about
alcoholism (I thought a person should drink like a
gentleman, and that's all), was saying a prayer for Bob. I
said, "God, I don't know anything about drinking, but I
told Bob that I was sure that if he lived this way of life, he
could quit drinking. Now you have to help me." Something said to me—I call it "guidance"—it was like a voice
in the top of my head—"Bob must not touch one drop of
alcohol." I knew that wasn't my thought. So I called Bob,
and said I had guidance for him—and this is very important. He came over at ten in the morning, and I told him
that my guidance was that he mustn't touch one drop of
alcohol. He was very disappointed, because he thought
guidance would mean seeing somebody or going some-
place. And then—and this is something very relevant—he

---

*According to Willard Hunter, group prayer on the knees was utilized in the
Oxford Group when the matter was considered very important, as in this
case. Hunter later attended an Oxford Group meeting in the Williams's home,
and said, "T. Henry, you know something about AA, don't you?"
"Sure do," he replied, "it started right here." He was pointing to the spot
on the living room carpet where Dr. Bob had made his surrender on his knees.

said, "Henrietta, I don't understand it. *Nobody* understands it." Now that was the state of the world when we were beginning. He said, "Some doctor has written a book about it, but he doesn't understand it. I don't like the stuff. I don't want to drink." I said, "Well, Bob, that is what I have been guided about." And that was the beginning of our meetings, long before Bill ever came.

Congressman Seiberling said he was away at boarding school during much of this period, but attended summer meetings at the Williams's home. His sister Dorothy remembers her mother telling about the discussion with Dr. Bob. "I remember how he kept saying, 'Nobody knows why we have to drink,' " Dorothy said in 1981. A bright, perceptive person who became an editor for *Life* magazine, Dorothy described AA's origins as an interesting building sequence that was "just stone upon stone." She agreed that an amazing process was at work in the situation: "There were just too many coincidences." Even her mother's sudden conviction that Bob shouldn't touch another drop seemed to be inspiration, because Henrietta had never really known anything about alcoholism. Yet the thought came to her mother, Dorothy said, "like a bolt out of the blue."[10]

Henrietta had said that this conversation with Dr. Bob was eleven weeks before Bill called her, but it may have been only two or three weeks before. Dr. Bob's plight was so much in her thoughts that Bill's telephone call, the Saturday before Mother's Day in May 1935, came as an answer to her prayers.

Henrietta always said that Bill introduced himself in this manner: "I'm from the Oxford Group and I'm a rum hound from New York." Bill, as was becoming his practice, conveyed the fact that he was now staying sober and had a need to talk with another alcoholic.

Henrietta's immediate response was, "Thank God!" She thought the call was really "manna from heaven" and she immediately invited Bill to come out to her home for dinner.

Bill Wilson's biography points out that it "may seem

remarkable that a woman alone with three teenage children would be so quick to invite a strange man into her home."[11] This is explained, however, by the strong bond of trust that existed among Oxford Group members.

Although Henrietta did not know it, the telephone call came at the moment Dr. Bob was at a low point. On this afternoon, he had arrived home drunk, delivered a potted plant to his wife as a Mother's Day gift, and then gone upstairs to sleep it off.

What followed, of course, was the first meeting of the two AA co-founders at Henrietta's home the next day. Dr. Bob, terribly hung over, could not eat the dinner Henrietta had prepared. He had arrived expecting to make a quick exit. Instead, he and Bill talked privately until nearly midnight, and the Smiths left with the hope that an answer to his drinking problem was in sight.

It was, although Dr. Bob needed one final bout with alcohol about a month later in order to become entirely willing to do whatever might be needed to recover. Then, as the Oxford Group had advised, he took his pride in hand and set out to make amends to those with whom he had been having difficulties. This was really a follow-up to the costly sharing he had made when he finally admitted to his fellow Oxford Groupers that he was a "silent" (or secret) drinker.

This was a portion of the sobriety process Dr. Bob Smith had already understood even before Bill Wilson arrived in Akron, although he had not been ready to carry it out. The message he received from Bill was the medical view: that he had a deadly, incurable malady from which he could never hope to recover if he persisted in taking so much as one drink.

Henrietta Seiberling, having introduced Bill and Dr. Bob, now took further steps to make sure that Bill stayed around long enough to help his new friend stay sober. This was the Oxford Group's fifth C, Continuance. Since Bill could no longer afford to stay at the Mayflower Hotel, then Akron's finest, she persuaded a wealthy neighbor to provide him a room at the

Portage Country Club, just down the road from her home. Even this assistance was an outgrowth of her Oxford Group change. Dorothy Seiberling remembered that the neighbor, a self-taught engineer named John Gammeter, was "rough, tough and swore a lot." But he had also been moved by the spiritual change that had taken place in Henrietta's life, Dorothy remembered in 1981. Bill stayed at the Portage for about two weeks. Despite his wretched financial condition, he even managed to play a few rounds of golf there.

In the meantime, Bill Wilson also joined Henrietta and the Smiths in the Wednesday evening Oxford Group meetings at the Williams home. This was another important development growing out of the 1933 rally. Bill and Dr. Bob did not have to go through the painful, laborious process of launching a regular group meeting. This was already in place, aided by nonalcoholic Oxford Group members who were deeply committed to the goal of helping Dr. Bob and other alcoholics. Bill Wilson, upon returning to New York City that fall and later encountering criticism and rejection at Calvary House (see Chapter Six), must have wished at times for the warmth and understanding of these Akron meetings. He developed the same kind of group setting in New York, but only after going through difficult trial-and-error sessions and facing other problems.

In a letter to Lois that summer, Bill mentioned Bud Firestone, whose recovery had started the fortunate chain of events in Akron. Bill didn't indicate that he met Firestone that summer, although the tire heir and his wife had taken an early role in promoting Oxford Group work in Ohio. Firestone's experience in the Oxford Group did help him become a more active executive in his father's company as well as a key person at St. Paul's Episcopal Church. It turned out that his 1931 meeting with Sam Shoemaker in the train compartment gave him another twenty years of useful life, and his brother Leonard remembered that Bud was very much at peace with himself when he died of cancer in 1951.

❧   ❧   ❧

Firestone's recovery, however, was only one of the threads that helped form the early alcoholic work in Akron. Years before Bill Wilson arrived in Akron, a man who came to be known as "Anonymous Number Three" was going through the painful process of "paying his dues" for admission to the exclusive fellowship of recovering alcoholics. He was Bill D., a gentle, folksy lawyer whose life was exemplary except for one problem: he went completely out of control while drinking and couldn't seem to stay away from the one drink that triggered it all. This was at a time when alcoholics were considered the worst of sinners, but Bill D. was actually a devout church member who believed in the precepts of his religion. He was happily married to the attractive woman he had courted while growing up in Kentucky, and he had put himself through law school by working in an Akron tire factory. Well-liked by everybody, he had even served as a city council member and financial director of an Akron suburb.

Bill D.'s wife, who was also named Henrietta, had the same confidence in the power of prayer that helped Henrietta Seiberling find guidance for Dr. Bob. Henrietta D. was not a member of the Oxford Group, but she had been praying for an answer to her husband's drinking problem. Unhappy with the response of their own minister, she had sought out the pastor of another church whose advice and prayers had given her the conviction that an answer would come.

Again, perfect timing and "coincidences" were at work. In late June 1935, Bill Wilson was living in the Smith home and Dr. Bob had taken his last drink and firmly embraced the Oxford Group program. The two men were beginning to work as a team in helping others. In seeking out alcoholics to help, Dr. Bob telephoned Akron City Hospital and learned about a drunken lawyer who was shackled to the bed after beating up a nurse during admission. The year was not half over, and yet Bill D. had been hospitalized eight times for intoxication.

Henrietta D. later said that when she met Bill Wilson and Dr. Bob for the first time, she knew immediately that her prayers had been answered. And so it proved to be, because Bill D. left the hospital a free man. He became an inspiration and friend to all who knew him, and he was a firm advocate of person-to-person contacts. Bill D.'s contribution to AA was at the local, group level, however, and he never had much confidence in the Big Book project and other measures designed to carry the message to the world. His personal story, for example, did not appear in the first edition of *Alcoholics Anonymous*, and was prepared only after Bill Wilson went to Akron, taped Bill D.'s recollections, and then wrote the story. It first appeared in the second edition, published a year after Bill D.'s death in 1954, and was retained in the third edition, published in 1976.

Following the successful sponsorship of Bill D., Dr. Bob and Anne Smith went on to bring many others into the early movement. It was largely their work that launched AA throughout the Midwest, including Cleveland, Toledo, Detroit, and other communities within driving distance of Akron. This Akron-based work had become so successful by 1938 that it was the focus of a special report prepared by Frank Amos for John D. Rockefeller, Jr. The purpose of the report was to seek Rockefeller's financial support of the movement (see Chapter Ten). Amos, then a New York advertising executive who later returned to Cambridge, Ohio, to run his family's newspaper, would become one of the Alcoholic Foundation's first trustees as well as a close friend of Bill Wilson.

Amos's report disclosed that of about 110 persons believed to be in the alcoholic recovery movement by then, at least seventy were in the Akron/Cleveland area. Interviewing other physicians and professionals in Akron, he found the highest praise for Dr. Bob as a competent surgeon and as a responsible person who had found a way to help others recover from alcoholism. He reported on Henrietta Seiberling's "unstinted admiration for Dr. Smith and his entire group who have

75

followed him," as well as that of the T. Henry Williamses, "who had become so impressed with the work of Smith and his associates that they turn over their home to them twice weekly for religious and social gatherings."[12]

Rockefeller, relying largely on Amos's fine report on the Akron movement and the recommendations of his associates, did agree to limited financial support. This facilitated the establishment of the Alcoholic Foundation and the preparation of the Big Book, *Alcoholics Anonymous*.

As much as anything, the Big Book project highlighted the differences between the Akron and New York AA movements. While Dr. Bob supported the Big Book plan, it had strong opposition in Akron and was approved there by only a small margin. "We're doing fine the way we are," was the attitude of many Akron members, and in truth they were.

Bill Wilson had a larger vision that was also supported by Dr. Bob. He wanted to give the AA message worldwide distribution. If Akron was the best proving ground for the early work, it's also true that it took Bill Wilson's work in New York City to make AA the international movement it has become today. He was fully prepared to give the Akron movement all due credit for its remarkable success. But he wanted to take steps that would carry the same program to other cities throughout the country, and the Big Book helped do that.

This effort was so successful that by 1948 the distant state of California surpassed Ohio in AA membership, a lead it has maintained ever since. But AA flourishes in Akron and other midwestern communities too, still carrying on the fine work that Dr. Bob, Anne, Henrietta Seiberling, and the T. Henry Williamses set in place in the early years. And, reflecting their Oxford Group heritage, the Akron/Cleveland groups still offer the Four Absolutes: Love, Honesty, Purity, and Unselfishness.

CHAPTER FIVE

Bill Wilson's Hot Flash

AA members sometimes talk—often with a bit of awe—about Bill Wilson's "hot flash" in New York City's Towns Hospital in 1934.

Since the remarks are at times made partly in jest, it's hard to determine whether most of today's AA members really believe that this landmark experience was, indeed, a true spiritual illumination of a high order. After all, it came to a man who was undergoing detoxification after years of savage drinking. It could also be attributed to chemical reaction from the drugs used in the "detox" process.

The most significant reference point for a sudden dramatic spiritual experience from Christian history is what happened to Saul of Tarsus on the Damascus Road sometime between A.D. 34 and 36. This transformed him from a man with murderous intent into the great Christian missionary, Saint Paul. Nobody has tried to confer sainthood on Wilson, but is there any evidence that he did undergo a "Damascus Road" type of change?

Bill Wilson always thought his 1934 experience was a true illumination. On some occasions, he referred people to the 1901 book *Cosmic Consciousness*, authored by a Canadian doctor named Richard Maurice Bucke.[1] As for Wilson's first awareness of this book, it must have come from an extensive quotation in William James's *The Varieties of Religious Experience*, which Wilson read while still a patient at Towns Hospital.

Why should a book about cosmic consciousness be considered as one of the spiritual roots of AA and the Twelve Steps? One reason is that the explanation, as presented by William James, helped Wilson partly understand what had happened to him. It opened his mind up to a spiritual reality that had previously been beyond his thoughts.

The experience was truly a hot flash, as searing and blinding as a streak of lightning across the sky. It had the effect of changing Bill Wilson's life in the barest part of a moment and setting him on the path that finally led to the founding of AA. It gave him a belief in God, or Higher Power, that never wavered despite much suffering in later years, including a recurring profound depression.

As Wilson put it in a 1956 letter, "With me, the original experience was so prodigious, the preview of destiny so intense, that I have never had any difficulty with doubts since that time. Even at my worst, and that has often been damn bad, the sense of the presence of God has never deserted me. That has pulled me through some awful jams. My doubts have been about myself, as a going human concern. Never has there been any question about the ultimate destiny of us all, or of God's justice and love."[2]

Bill Wilson had this hot flash shortly after a visit by his friend and sponsor, Ebby. Ebby had told him about the main suggestions of the Oxford Group program for spiritual change, which included deep soul-searching or personal inventory and a complete willingness to accept God's guidance and direction. Here's how Wilson described what happened to him:

> These were revolutionary and drastic proposals, but the moment I fully accepted them, the effect was electric. There was a sense of victory, followed by such a peace and serenity as I had never known. There was utter confidence. I felt lifted up, as though the great

clean wind of a mountain top blew through and
through. God comes to most men gradually, but His
impact on me was sudden and profound.[3]

Cosmic consciousness is discussed in detail in Richard
Bucke's book, but here's William James's description as Wilson
would have read it shortly after undergoing his own remarkable
experience. Bucke, already a respected person in his profession, had been visiting in London in 1872, when the following experience came to him:

I had spent the evening in a great city, with two
friends, reading and discussing poetry and philosophy.
We parted at midnight. I had a long drive in a hansom
to my lodging. My mind, deeply under the influence
of the ideas, images, and emotions called up by the
reading and talk, was calm and peaceful. I was in a state
of quiet, almost passive enjoyment, not actually thinking, but letting ideas, images, and emotions flow of
themselves, as it were, through my mind. All at once,
without warning of any kind, I found myself wrapped
in a flame-colored cloud. For an instant I thought of
fire, an immense conflagration somewhere close by in
that great city; the next, I knew that the fire was within
myself. Directly afterward there came upon me a sense
of exultation, of immense joyousness accompanied or
immediately followed by an intellectual illumination impossible to describe. Among other things, I did not
merely come to believe, but I saw that the universe is
not composed of dead matter, but is, on the contrary,
a living Presence; I became conscious in myself of eternal life. It was not a conviction that I would have eternal
life, but a consciousness that I possessed eternal life
then: I saw that all men are immortal; that the cosmic
order is such that without any peradventure all things
work together for the good of each and all; that the
foundation principle of the world, of all the worlds,

is what we call love, and that the happiness of each
and all is in the long run absolutely certain. The vision
lasted a few seconds and was gone; but the memory
of it and the sense of the reality of what it taught has
remained during the quarter of a century which has
since elapsed. I knew that what the vision showed was
true. I had attained to a point of view from which I saw
that it must be true. That view, that conviction, I may
say that consciousness, has never, even during periods
of the deepest depression, been lost.[4]

Was this a true experience in God-consciousness or was it
simply an astonishing delusion? It has been viewed both ways
in scientific literature. As a religious experience, it is very close
to similar reports from others who have undergone sudden
and profound changes in their lives. Many religious leaders
have had such experiences, although their followers might not
be willing to accept Bucke's account as authentic because it is
not related to their doctrines.

But it was the scientific side of Bucke's mind that helped him
explain his experience and target the elements that ranked it
as cosmic consciousness. He saw these points, explained in
the following quotations, as common to the fifty or so case
histories he studied:

- *Subjective Light.* "The person, suddenly, without warning,
  has a sense of being immersed in a flame, or rose-colored
  cloud, or perhaps rather a sense that the mind is itself filled
  with such a cloud of haze."
- *Great Joy.* "At the same instant he is, as it were, bathed in
  an emotion of joy, assurance, triumph, 'salvation.' "
- *Intellectual Illumination with Moral Elevation.* "Simultaneously
  or instantly following the above sense and emotional experiences there comes to the person an intellectual illumination
  quite impossible to describe. . . . He sees. . .that the foundation
  principle of the world is what we call love, and that the happiness of every individual is in the long run absolutely certain."

- *A Sense of Immortality.* "With illumination the fear of death which haunts so many men and women at times all their lives falls off like an old cloak—not, however, as a result of reasoning—it simply vanishes."[5]

The feature that makes Bucke's account so useful is that it parallels William James's later effort in *The Varieties of Religious Experience.* While both Bucke and James had had personal spiritual experiences, they tried to "stand outside" themselves to sort out the common points that could tie together many such experiences. This is about the only way this subject can be approached. The study of spiritual or religious experiences, like much of the social sciences, does not have the advantage of "repeatable laboratory experiments." Whatever happens to the individual is by its very nature a once-in-a-lifetime event and depends on the special conditions of the time. There is no way, for example, that science could re-create the feelings and conditions that surrounded Paul's conversion on the Damascus Road or, for that matter, the many conversions of modern times. Bill Wilson often explained that complete "ego deflation at depth" preceded his illumination. But the illumination itself so changed his mind that any future ego deflation would also have a different character.

In Bill Wilson's case, it was the suddenness of the change that overwhelmed him and left such a lasting effect. At first, this led him to believe that other alcoholics needed an identical experience in order to achieve sobriety. Later he decided that the same results occurred more gradually for others, and he would gently explain to them that their own longer-term spiritual growth was really the same experience stretched out over time. This explanation even helped support the idea of changing "spiritual experience" to "spiritual awakening" in the Twelfth Step. And it was a concept important enough to be added to the second edition of *Alcoholics Anonymous* as Appendix II, "Spiritual Experience."

Bucke believed that only certain cases could truly be termed *cosmic consciousness.* His theory was based on the belief that humans really have available three planes of consciousness. The most basic is Simple Consciousness, which human beings share with animals. The next plane is Self Consciousness, an advanced state that sets humans above the animals and, in effect, gives humankind dominion over the earth as a result of high intelligence, use of tools, and abstract reasoning powers. Wonderful as it is, however, Self Consciousness doesn't meet our deepest needs or solve our most perplexing problems. It cannot prepare us for our true destiny. This is the role of the third plane, or Cosmic Consciousness.

People who possess this new sense will bring about a true paradise on earth, Bucke believed. As he saw it, Cosmic Conscious people would in reality be a new race, bringing a new heaven and a new earth and making all things new. The isolated individuals who have felt the Cosmic Sense in the past have been the spiritual leaders we honor in the present time, he believed. They are also "the first faint beginnings of another race, walking the earth and breathing the air with us, but at the same time walking another earth and breathing another air of which we know little or nothing, but which is, all the same, our spiritual life. . . . This new race is in the act of being born from us, and in the near future it will occupy and possess the earth."[6]

In Bucke's view, the individuals of the past whose Cosmic Sense led them to profound spiritual achievements included Buddha, Jesus, Isaiah, Moses, Mohammed, and Paul. He also cited writers and poets such as Dante, Francis Bacon, and Walt Whitman. As a close friend of Whitman, Bucke believed that the poet's Cosmic Sense was greater than most others'.

But Bucke was not a religious person in the conventional sense, and his writings did not cover the less spectacular spiritual experiences that had come to some of the more practical Christian reformers of that era like Charles Finney, Dwight L. Moody, or William Booth. He was inclined to look at the universe and creation as a deist or even a humanist skeptic might see it—that is, believing in some sort of God, First Cause, or Universal Presence, but having no active program for enhancing and strengthening the spiritual consciousness he had discovered and identified.

It seems logical, for example, to believe that Frank Buchman's experience at Keswick was a Cosmic Illumination of some sort. During that brief experience, it was Buchman's swift change in thought and feeling that then helped set the course of his entire life and led others to similar experiences. Like most evangelicals, Buchman and the Oxford Group said their activity was "leading people to Christ." But this was a Christ more like AA's Higher Power, who was really an In-dwelling Presence that also transforms lives and then supports this change by supplying continuous Guidance, Strength, and Power.

The Christian evangelicals and fundamentalists could probably produce hundreds of cases that border on cosmic consciousness, although they would not be comfortable with that term. One most remarkable experience came to a future Salvation Army officer named Samuel Logan Brengle in 1885, more than ten years after Bucke had his illumination in London.

Brengle is still honored in The Salvation Army as one of the organization's outstanding missionaries who carried the work to many countries. But he was a student at Boston Theological Seminary when he had his great spiritual experience. He had gone through a period of earnest soul-searching and deep prayer. Finally he reached a point of complete surrender. This was followed by an experience that still goes by the terms *Sanctification* and *Holiness* in The Salvation Army:

> I awoke that morning hungering and thirsting just to live this life of fellowship with God, never again to sin in thought or word or deed against Him, with an unmeasurable desire to be a holy man, acceptable unto God.... (I received) such a blessing as I never had dreamed a man could have this side of heaven.... It was a heaven of love that came into my heart. My soul

melted like wax before fire. . . . Every ambition for self
was now gone. The pure flame of love burned it like
a blazing fire would burn a moth.

I walked out over Boston Commons before breakfast,
weeping for joy and praising God. Oh, how I loved!
In that hour I knew Jesus, and I loved Him till it seemed
my heart would break with love. I was filled with love
for all His creatures. I heard the little sparrows chat-
tering; I loved them. I saw a little worm wriggling across
my path; I stepped over it; I didn't want to hurt
any living thing. I loved the dogs, I loved the horses, I
loved the little urchins on the street. . . . I loved the
whole world![7]

Brengle, like Bucke, was caught up in the conviction that Love
is the foundation of all Creation. This sweeping conversion experience soon led Brengle to choose The Salvation Army rather
than service as a minister in an affluent church. He was sent
to an officers' training school, where he surpassed most of the
other cadets in education and intelligence. Despite his illustrious background, one of the first assignments given him was
cleaning the other cadets' shoes in a dark cellar. At first resentful, Brengle then began to practice his beliefs by praying for
each lad whose shoes he cleaned. Like Brother Lawrence centuries before him, Brengle transformed this bleak assignment
into a joyous spiritual experience. People who study his life
feel that this single experience helped prepare him to become
The Salvation Army's great *Holiness* missionary.

Brengle's experience parallels those reported from many
evangelical revivals. People who have had these experiences
often speak of the great joy their faith has given them. "Light"
is frequently mentioned. And of course, to be real, such experience is always accompanied by a great love of humanity,
the marvelous feeling of general goodwill that Christian
theologians signify with the Greek term *agape.*

These experiences can come in other ways, however, and one

such emotion of general goodwill was reported by Sir Francis Younghusband (1863-1942), a distinguished British Army Officer and explorer who was widely known in his day as an author and mystic:

> I had a curious sense of being literally in love with the world. There is no other way in which I can express what I then felt. I felt as if I could hardly contain myself for the love which was bursting within me. It seemed to me as if the world itself were nothing but love. . . . At the back. . .of things I was certain was love—and not merely placid benevolence, but active, fervent, devoted love, and nothing less.[8]

Dr. Cecil Osborne, a minister who did important work with inspirational therapy groups on the West Coast, described a similar experience of his own: "Love, I sensed, was at the heart of everything, and God was in everything, and everything was in God, and God was inexpressible love."

Osborne went on to describe an experience in which the ordinary things of the world appeared amazingly beautiful. He found himself loving total strangers, and feeling warmth and affection in everyone. "We were all one, and there was no barrier between us," he wrote. "They were just parts of God's glorious, wonderful, joyous, loving universe, and they were beautiful."[9]

There have undoubtedly been thousands of experiences like Bill Wilson's. They tell of a different world that has always been here, but can only be felt by people who have become open to experience it. The prideful, self-important person is not likely to have such an experience until events humble him into a state of willingness. Willingness is apparently the key to spiritual experience, just as AA members also believe it to be the key to real sobriety. As Bill Wilson described it, the essential requirements for the new relationship with his Creator were "belief in the power of God, plus enough willingness, honesty and humility to establish and maintain the new order of

85

things." The price to be paid for this was "the destruction of self-centeredness. I must turn in all things to the Father of Light who presides over us all."[10]

People who are undergoing such experiences are portrayed in biblical terms as "renewing their strength, mounting up with wings as eagles; they shall run, and not be weary; and they shall walk, and not faint" (Isaiah 40:31). Bill Wilson described his hot flash as giving him utter confidence and "a greater peace and serenity as he had never known."[11]

The danger of such an exalted emotional state, for alcoholics, is that the feelings can parallel the false joys and ecstasies that can come from drinking and drugging. One alcoholic delusion is that it might somehow be possible to live continuously in such a blissful state. An alcoholic who finds moments of joyous exultation in sobriety is bound to demand even stronger and more satisfying experiences. It is not by chance that spiritual people have been called "God-intoxicated" or that the first-century Christians were suspected of being drunk following Pentecost, as described in Acts in the New Testament.

Norman Vincent Peale warns, however, that no one can permanently live in such exalted emotional heights. He does believe that this spiritual power will help sustain a person in day-by-day situations, providing strength and emotional uplift to keep going even when one is up against things that used to be difficult and monotonous.[12]

For Bill Wilson and AA, the moment of illumination supplied at least three important contributions. One result was making Bill Wilson a changed (or "converted") man, with new confidence, new faith, and new goals.

A second effect of the Cosmic experience was the conviction that a Source of Power was continuously at hand to aid any open-minded person in the ordinary business of living. Bill Wilson had occasional personal troubles in maintaining his own conscious contact with this Higher Power in the years to come. Yet he was steadfast in helping others find spiritual growth by following the path outlined in the Twelve Steps.

The third great result of Bill's hot flash was that he immediately began to think of ways that a similar experience could benefit others. "While I lay in the hospital the thought came that there were thousands of hopeless alcoholics who might be glad to have what had been so freely given me," he later wrote. "Perhaps I could help some of them. They in turn might work with others."[13]

This single thought, we know today, started a process of recovery for millions of alcoholics. But why did Bill Wilson think about helping others rather than using his newfound power to rebuild his shattered business career and reach other personal objectives? He was admittedly a generous, usually kind person even in the worst of his drinking. He also possessed, however, a powerful, driving ambition that had been an engine of destruction in his life. What was there about the hot flash that transformed him into a true benefactor of humankind rather than just another hustler in search of renewed business success?

Bucke had argued that using the power for the benefit of the human race is the only decision permitted in Cosmic Consciousness. A great moral elevation is part of the experience. Were it not so, he insisted, the intellectual illumination that accompanies the new consciousness would make its subjects, in effect, demons who would end by destroying the world. Bucke argued, too, that selfish use of this higher power would cause a person to fall.[14]

But Bill Wilson wouldn't have read this additional explanation until years later. The example of helping others was freely given to him by Ebby and the Oxford Group. Bill Wilson's talent was in adapting the Oxford Group principles to the special needs of alcoholics. In time, he added ideas gleaned from the early experiences of other alcoholics in the pioneering AA groups.

Though he also talked freely about his spiritual experience with people who were sincerely interested, Wilson always took the broad view that there were many paths to such growth.

His was clearly a kind of "born-again" experience, but he did not think adherence to the Christian religion was a prerequisite for such an event in one's life. "Christ is, of course, the leading figure to me," he wrote to an AA member. "Yet I have never been able to receive complete assurance that He was one hundred percent God. I seem to be just as comfortable with the figure of ninety-nine percent. I know that from a conservative Christian point of view, this is a terrific heresy. But it must be remembered that I had no childhood conditioning in religion at all. I quit Congregational Sunday School at eleven because they asked me to sign a Temperance pledge. So, what shall I do? Of course I don't know—except to try to be open-minded." He added, "I do think it imperative that neither my theological views nor those of Dr. Bob ever have any appreciable influence on AA. That would only create another competing religion. Of these, we certainly have enough already."[15]

To the end of his days, Bill Wilson considered himself "a shopper at the theological pie counter." But true to Bucke's description of the experience, Bill believed that personal immortality "has the certainty of knowledge through evidence." His hot flash, which he considered a fleeting glimpse of ultimate destiny, was a way of previewing this eternal future in the "Father's house of many mansions."[16]

And along the way, of course, it helped get a lot of drunks sober!

Breaking with the Oxford Group

Early in 1937, the Oxford Groups sponsored a major house party at the Hotel Thayer in West Point, New York. While *house party* also described smaller group meetings, the West Point gathering was a larger affair, perhaps more like an AA state or regional conference might be today.

Lois Wilson remembered that an Oxford Group woman drove her and two friends to West Point, where Bill met them. As it turned out, the Hotel Thayer meeting was the last large house party they attended. By that summer, both Bill and Lois had stopped attending the Oxford Group meetings. They had attended two meetings weekly in New York for two and one-half years.

In later years, their departure became viewed, even by Bill Wilson, as "a break with the Oxford Group." He would explain that the New York AA members left the Oxford Group in 1937, while the Akron people continued to identify themselves as Oxford Groupers until 1939. He would add, however, that it was only the close tie with T. Henry and Clarace Williams, including weekly meetings in their home, that kept the Akron members in the Oxford Group fold for an additional two years. Wilson's gratitude to the Williamses was boundless, in fact, and he consistently expressed his appreciation to them in print and conversation long after the Akron members had launched their own meeting elsewhere.

In the New York City area, however, Bill Wilson and the

band of recovering alcoholics he assembled had been criticized for holding special "drunks-only" meetings. This criticism had come from Jack Smith, Sam Shoemaker's assistant and close friend. The Wilsons had been holding these meetings for alcoholics in their home in Brooklyn, and this gradually fanned out to become the New York City area's AA movement. But Jack Smith and other Oxford Group leaders disapproved of it, and Smith even alluded to the special meetings as being "held surreptitiously behind Mrs. Jones's barn." Lois Wilson said that the atmosphere of the Oxford Group became slightly chilly toward her and Bill, and near the end of 1935 the leaders at Calvary Mission barred their alcoholic residents from attending the meetings at the Wilson home.[1]

Where was Sam Shoemaker while all this was happening? While neither Bill nor Lois ever blamed Shoemaker for these rebuffs, he certainly must have agreed with his assistant that the special meetings were wrong. It was one of the rejections that eventually led Bill to leave the Oxford Group. It's a measure of Shoemaker's humility, however, that he later apologized for this in a personal letter. Long after Shoemaker had broken with the Oxford Group, he wrote to Bill: "If you ever write the story of AA's early connection with Calvary, I think it ought to be said in all honesty that we were coached in the feeling that you were off on your own spur, trying to do something by yourself, and out of the mainstream of the work. You got your inspiration from those early days, but you didn't get much encouragement from any of us, and for my own part in that stupid desire to control the Spirit, as He manifested Himself in individual people like yourself, I am heartily sorry and ashamed."[2]

Bob Scott, an Oxford Group member who later became a professor of jurisprudence at Michigan State University, recalled an incident at the Hotel Thayer meeting that may have contributed to the break. According to Scott, a proposal was made to have a separate division in the Oxford Group for alcoholics. "This proposal was not looked on too kindly," Scott recalled.[3]

Bill Wilson was not the one who voiced that proposal at the West Point meeting, but he certainly must have been in sympathy with it. The proposal does suggest that recovering alcoholics in the Oxford Group did view their problem as being "special" and felt they needed meetings focusing on alcoholism.

According to Lois Wilson, the Oxford Groupers also invoked one of their special terms to convey their view of special work with alcoholism. She and Bill were "not maximum," they had been told at Calvary House. "This not only hurt us but left us disappointed in the group's leadership," she recalled.[4]

Willard Hunter said that Buchman and other Oxford Groupers used the term *maximum* to identify performance they considered to be tops. Buchman thought that alcoholism was only part of what was wrong in the world, Hunter said, and as already noted, he quoted Frank Buchman as saying, "We also have drunken nations on our hands." When pressed to pinpoint just when and why Buchman had made such a statement, Hunter decided it may have come in 1939, when Akron AA members were separating from the Oxford Group. Hunter believes that T. Henry Williams, the nonalcoholic Oxford Group member who had hosted the early Akron meetings in his home, would have discussed the split with Buchman. And Buchman, now preoccupied with larger issues, may have even been relieved that the alcoholics were choosing a separate path.[5]

Whatever the circumstances, this statement that "we have drunken nations on our hands" clearly defined the Oxford Group's nation-changing, peace-seeking role as being the more urgent objective. Peace did, indeed, become Buchman's overriding concern as the 1930s wore on and the European nations began re-arming to counter the threat posed by Nazi Germany. It was this emphasis on re-arming militarily, in fact, that helped inspire Buchman with *Moral* Re-Armament, the new name applied to his movement after 1938.

Buchman was said to have conceived the idea of Moral Re-Armament while spending a few days in a hideaway at Freudenstadt, in Germany's Black Forest, during the spring of 1938. "One day as he was walking in a shady lane," Hunter wrote, "the thought came to him, 'Moral and spiritual re-armament, the next step.' " (Hunter added that the lane was subsequently named "Frank Buchman Way" by town authorities, and that the nearby Waldlust Hotel was where Buchman was to die twenty-three years later.)[6]

It's another of those remarkable "coincidences" that 1938 was the year of a major directional change for the Oxford Group and Frank Buchman, because it turned out to be a key year, too, for the future Alcoholics Anonymous and Bill Wilson. Wilson, who had struggled unsuccessfully to rebuild a Wall Street career, later marked 1938 as the year he began devoting himself full time to the molding of AA. The writing of the AA Big Book was launched that year, and the first use of the term *Alcoholics Anonymous* surfaced in the summer of 1938. So at the very time the Oxford Group was moving into a more ex-pansive phase as MRA, the alcoholics who had found help in that fellowship were moving in another direction as a small-group movement devoted exclusively to helping people with alcoholic problems.

The emerging AA fellowship, though probably unknowingly, was also taking on the practice of anonymity that Frank Buchman had employed in the early 1920s and then abandoned. By 1939, the man who had been only "F.B." six-teen years earlier in Harold Begbie's *More Twice-Born Men* was the star of a mass Hollywood Bowl meeting that drew thirty thousand people and turned away another ten thousand for lack of seating. And for the next twenty-two years, until his death in 1961, Frank Buchman would be associated with well-publicized MRA meetings, with considerable press attention to participation by prominent, influential people.

AA's principle of anonymity, as it developed in the beginning, was simply a method of assuring alcoholic prospects that their association with the fellowship would be kept in confidence. Clarence S., one of the AA founding members in Cleveland, even insisted that it had been intended only to protect other members. A member should be free to publicly reveal his own AA identity, Clarence thought, and he did so in a 1942 letter to the editor.[7]

Bill Wilson shared this view at one time. He was publicly identified, photographs and all, as an AA member in the early 1940s. He later began to feel that such publicity was a mistake that would eventually damage AA and perhaps even tear it apart. He recovered his own anonymity as Bill W. and urged other members to do the same. He sealed the idea of personal anonymity in the Eleventh and Twelfth traditions, which were formally adopted along with the other AA traditions at the First International Convention in 1950.

The Eleventh Tradition, expressing the public relations policy of attraction rather than promotion, advises personal anonymity at the public media level. The Twelfth Tradition goes further, however, by declaring anonymity to be the "spiritual foundation of all our traditions, ever reminding us to place principles before personalities." Though there was probably no direct connection, this idea was surprisingly close to the same principle that had moved Frank Buchman to maintain anonymity in the book *More Twice-Born Men*.

It's doubtful that Bill Wilson and the alcoholics who joined him had even been missed when they left the Oxford Group in 1937. A few Oxford Group people romanticized this split later on by depicting an imaginary discussion in which Buchman gave Wilson his blessing in going forth to help alcoholics. Oxford Group members said they had wanted Wilson to help "change" his former Wall Street associates. Bill Wilson had so little standing on Wall Street, however, that he could not obtain a job there in his former capacity as a broker. He would hardly have been in any position to carry out such missionary efforts.

The 1939 separation from the Oxford Group by the Akron alcoholics was painful, but largely because of the affection and gratitude Dr. Bob Smith and others felt for the Williamses. For several years, the Williamses had supported the meetings.

"They purchased a lot of extra chairs, served many suppers, and stood for much wear and tear on their house too," Bill Wilson once recalled. "We alcoholics did not pay a cent. T. Henry and Clarace sacrificed a great amount of time and some money. If they had not done so, there could not have been any meeting."[8]

Dr. Bob's biography discloses that pressures for making such a separation had been mounting among Akron members, although some opposed it. With Alcoholics Anonymous now clearly moving ahead under its own name in 1939, it was restrictive to have a meeting that was still tied to the Oxford Group, however benevolent the Williamses might have been. In Cleveland, for example, the movement had started meeting separately in May 1939 as Alcoholics Anonymous, with no mention of the Oxford Group. It was inevitable that the parent group in nearby Akron would make the same separation, and they did so in November or December of 1939.

One reason given for the separation—perhaps to help spare the Williams's feelings—was that more room was needed for the growing membership. But since the group temporarily met in Dr. Bob's house, which was smaller than the Williams's fine home, this was simply a tactful excuse. The real reason for the split was that the alcoholics felt they needed their own meeting, free of any Oxford Group ties. Dr. Bob's biography even notes that he had felt hampered by this Oxford Group connection. Writing to Bill Wilson on January 2, 1940, he said, "Have definitely shaken off the shackles of the Oxford Group and are meeting at my house for the time being. Had 74 Wednesday in my little house, but shall get a hall soon."[9]

This marked the complete separation of AA from the Oxford Group. Except for T. Henry and Clarace Williams, it's doubtful that anybody in the new Moral Re-Armament organization regretted the departure of fewer than one hundred alcoholics from the Midwest. Though Buchman was said to have addressed the Akron alcoholic group in 1938, he took no interest in the new society and apparently never mentioned it in his speeches and writings.

But the separation continued to create problems for Bill Wilson when AA members inquired about it. A recurrent question was about the Four Absolutes, which survived in the Cleveland/Akron area but were not included in the formal program and literature of AA World Services. Bill Wilson's answer was often that Absolutes—Purity, Honesty, Unselfishness, Love—couldn't be imposed on alcoholics. These were ideas that had to be fed to alcoholics with teaspoons rather than by buckets, he said.[10] At other times, he explained that the four concepts were included or implied in the Twelve Steps.

There's good reason to believe, however, that Bill Wilson's main reason for passing over the Absolutes is that they would have closely identified the AA fellowship with Moral Re-Armament and Frank Buchman. It disturbed him that the Oxford Group had been falling fast in the public's favor. He was even more concerned about scattered criticisms of the Group from the Roman Catholic church, and it was rumored that the Pope might forbid Catholics to attend Oxford Group meetings.

True or not, such a rumor was taken seriously. Wilson was particularly sensitive to the Catholic response. Despite the fact that AA used religious principles and terms—or perhaps because of it—Wilson had always sought out words and practices that could be accepted by alcoholics of any faith. He had even sent a copy of the AA Big Book to Catholic diocesan headquarters in New York for review before publication. While this would seem to be excessive caution in today's climate, it was a prudent move in 1939, when Catholic church authority carried more weight with individual Catholics than it does today. Any official Catholic disapproval of AA would have been a terrible blow, and Wilson took all necessary steps to avoid such a problem. His view was always that any problems of this kind would condemn still-suffering alcoholics to an early death and must be avoided at all costs.

In this respect, Bill Wilson took a position that sharply contrasted with Frank Buchman's approach. Both advocated the need for finding spiritual answers by seeking God's guidance, but Wilson was more likely to check any guidance he received with trusted friends. For him, strong negative or positive feedback and the helpful comments of others were also forms of guidance. Buchman often disregarded negative feedback, and even believed that criticism was simply part of the persecution that a true Christian believer must expect in the world.

Buchman's strong belief in his guidance as coming directly from God—even when it might prove wrong—created problems for his associates. It caused some of them, including Sam Shoemaker, to break with him on a permanent basis. It was also a surprising stance for a man whose humble admission of being wrong had sparked his spiritual transformation in 1908.

The most damaging incident by far was the Buchman newspaper interview in August 1936, resulting in a story that portrayed him as a Hitler sympathizer. Ironically, this came during a year that saw Buchman on the cover of *Time* magazine and also brought the Oxford Group high praise growing out of its large meeting in the Berkshires.

Bill Wilson summarized the reasons for breaking with the Oxford Group, in an October 30, 1940, letter. One of his points was that the Group's agressive evangelism didn't seem to work for "neurotics of our hue," though he conceded it may have been absolutely vital to the success of the Oxford Group. He also thought the Group used coercive tactics that caused resentments. He noted too that excessive personal publicity or prominence was found to be bad (for alcoholics). Additionally, he cited the misunderstanding with the Catholic church and the difficulties with the guidance principle. He also suggested that the principles of tolerance and love had to be emphasized much more in actual practice than they were in the Oxford Group—especially tolerance. This comment veered closer to criticism than Wilson usually ventured, but his own experience with the Oxford Group was still fairly recent in 1940. These views were primarily expressed in private correspondence, but Bill repeated them many times and they were listed in his biography, *Pass It On* (pp. 171-173).

A few months later, Bill Wilson also sought to keep any mention of the Oxford Group out of the upcoming *Saturday Evening Post* article that would cause the fellowship's membership to skyrocket. Jack Alexander sent the manuscript to Wilson for clearance, but refused to omit at least a small reference to the Group. This effort to exclude the Group completely from any public mention shows how deeply Bill Wilson had come to feel about the subject. But as he had said in his 1940 letter, he didn't publicly acknowledge a very real debt of gratitude to the Oxford Group because "unfortunately, a vast and sometimes unreasoning prejudice exists all over this country against the Oxford Group and its successor MRA. My dilemma is that if I make such an acknowledgement, I may establish a connection between the O.G. and Alcoholics Anonymous which does not exist at the present time. I had to ask myself which was the more important: that the O.G. receive credit and that I have the pleasure of so discharging my debt of gratitude, or that alcoholics everywhere have the best possible chance to stay alive regardless of who gets credit."[11]

But the Oxford Group reference in Jack Alexander's article apparently was either overlooked or carried no weight with the public. AA went on to enjoy astonishing growth and success under its own name, while the Oxford Group—now rechristened MRA—pursued the new course it had chosen. In leading MRA until his death in 1961, Frank Buchman continued to generate a swirl of controversy, although most of his press notices were favorable. He was indeed a controversial man, and his most recent biography, a well-documented account by Garth Lean, even begins with a short chapter titled "The Buchman Controversy." Lean, himself a Buchman intimate since 1932, called Frank Buchman "a man who set out to remake the world. That must be said at the outset," Lean explained, "because it is only possible to understand Frank Buchman in the context of that aim. Everything he did in his adult life was a part of it, and scarcely anything he did could, in his eyes, be separated from it. That aim conditioned where and how he lived, how he approached people and situations, and what he did from hour to hour."[12]

MRA declined in numbers and influence following Buchman's death and the untimely passing, in 1965, of Peter Howard, his successor as MRA's leader. The society is headquartered in Caux, Switzerland, where it still attracts loyal members to its summer meetings and other events. Its ideology continues to be based on the Four Absolutes and it still affirms Buchman's goal of remaking the world by changing individual lives.

Now that more than three decades have passed since Buchman's death, it is easy to look critically at his MRA involvement and to conclude that the society never succeeded in creating the peaceful world Buchman had in mind. But no other person or movement has been able to achieve that goal either, though many have tried. Even if Buchman could not reach that goal in his lifetime, he still may have planted seeds that will someday create a world closer to his dreams. What's astonishing about his life is the number of people and movements he influenced. Much of this work and influence still goes on in many forms, some of it by people who never suspect how much they owe to Buchman.

The "Buchman Controversy" will eventually disappear. What can never disappear are the principles Buchman pulled out of first-century Christianity and put to practical use: surrendering one's will to God; sharing one's experience, strength, and hope with others; practicing fellowship with others; seeking daily guidance through quiet times of meditation and prayer; making restitution for any wrongs; and "witnessing"—carrying the good news of all this to others. Nobody really should doubt that if these principles—what Bill Wilson called the "common property of mankind"—are widely and sincerely used, the world will be remade. The growing Twelve Step movement, with roots reaching back through Buchman's early work to draw on these principles, is certainly having a major impact on millions of peoples' lives throughout the world today.

In a smaller way, the early members of AA believed it was already happening for them: "Most of us feel we need look no further for Utopia," Bill Wilson wrote in 1939. "We have it with us right here and now. Each day my friend's simple talk in our kitchen multiplies itself in a widening circle of peace on earth and good will to men."[13]

CHAPTER SEVEN

Mutual Self-Help Ideas Were in the Air

AA's spiritual roots may be ancient and its reach has become international, but the society itself is clearly an American invention. As one member put it, "You couldn't possibly be more American than having a Bill Wilson and a Bob Smith as co-founders." AA is very much in line with an American practice of forming mutual self-help associations that have been around since the country's beginnings.

Some people think the self-help idea started with Ben Franklin's moralistic writings during Revolutionary times. It was certainly well in place by 1831, when the French statesman and writer Alexis de Tocqueville arrived for a visit that inspired him to write *Democracy in America.*

The societies he saw everywhere in the new nation amazed Tocqueville. "As soon as several of the inhabitants of the United States have taken up an opinion or a feeling which they wish to promote in the world," Tocqueville wrote, "they look out for mutual assistance; and as soon as they have found each other out, they combine. From that moment they are no longer isolated men, but a power seen from afar, whose actions serve for an example, and whose language is listened to."

Tocqueville's comments carried a marvelous reference to drinking and abstinence. He noted that he had thought it "more like a joke than a serious engagement" when first hearing that a hundred thousand men in the United States "had bound themselves publicly to abstain from spiritous liquors." At first, he couldn't understand why these temperate citizens couldn't just content themselves with drinking water by their own firesides.

Tocqueville realized, however, that such an association—he was obviously referring to forerunners of the Washingtonian movement—was necessary for mutual support in promoting *temperance,* a term then almost synonymous with AA's current use of *sobriety.* He went on to say that such a movement could not have developed in his own country, where the citizens would have simply looked to the French government for a solution. "Nothing, in my opinion, is more deserving of our attention than the intellectual and moral associations of America," he added, explaining that such societies were perhaps even more necessary to the American people than political and industrial associations. "If men are to remain civilized, or to become so," he concluded, "the art of associating together must grow and improve in the same ratio in which the equality of conditions is increased."[1]

As Tocqueville might have predicted, the art of associating together did grow and improve in America following his brief visit here. By the 1920s and 1930s, when AA was in its prebirthing stages, the Oxford Group was the outstanding mutual self-help organization. But the idea of forming as a society or group to solve common problems was a major part of American life and many religious groups. Service clubs, youth organizations, church training programs, and self-improvement systems such as the Coué, Toastmasters, and Dale Carnegie methods all supported the idea of helping oneself and banding together for this constructive purpose. Such ideas were very much in the air.

For this reason, it was not surprising that a similar idea took root with Bill Wilson following his remarkable spiritual experience at Towns Hospital in late 1934. "While I lay in the hospital the thought came that there were thousands of hopeless alcoholics who might be glad to have what had been so freely given me. Perhaps I could help some of them. They in turn might work with others," Wilson wrote.[2]

This comes across today as a preview of the future AA society. It could have seemed remarkably conceited to many people. Why did Bill Wilson—a man who hadn't made his own living for five years—think he had any chance to make an impression in the world fight against alcoholism?

One reason was certainly in the success of the fellowship that had helped him. The Oxford Group, as a spiritual society, exemplified the idea of helping oneself by providing inspirational help to others. And Wilson had been sponsored by a friend, Ebby, who was destitute and living in a mission. This made it clear that one didn't need financial resources to begin helping others.

Another reason for Wilson's vision of a helping society, however, is that general ideas along the same lines were woven into his Vermont upbringing. They were part of the American scene, and had been on the scene for a long time. Again, synchronicity seemed to be at work; these self-help and mutual support ideas had been coming together for more than a century. And in the mid-1930s, when Wilson set out on his quest, it was already accepted in America that ordinary people could help themselves and others in astonishing ways.

The mutual self-help movements took many forms, some calling themselves religious or spiritual, others merely being secular organizations of people with common interests. In some ways, they were modern extensions of the community barn raisings and other helping ventures from rural communities in early American life. And many of those that seemed closely related to AA as it finally developed were eventually to be identified with the "pop" psychology movement that shows no signs of abating today.

It is certain, too, that the early AA movement acquired a few ideas from the Christian Science and New Thought teachings, which William James called "mind-cure" in *The Varieties of Religious Experience.*

Like the Oxford Group, none of these movements worked all the time for everybody who sought help for personal problems. But as James noted about some religions, they worked when certain conditions were met. He apparently believed that the same process was at work no matter what it was called: The individual becomes willing to give up the old self or the old ways, becomes committed to the new way of life, and the answers come. James called this "surrender" the "way to success." He believed it worked this way: "Give up the feeling of responsibility, let go your hold, resign the care of your destiny to higher powers, be genuinely indifferent as to what becomes of it all, and you will find not only that you gain a perfect inward relief, but often also, in addition, the particular goods you sincerely thought you were re- nouncing."[3] It's not hard to see that this same idea was trans- ferred to AA as "Surrendering to Win" (which a college professor listed as one of four great paradoxes of AA in the second edition of *Alcoholics Anonymous*).[4]

Did Christian Science teachings have anything to do with the forming of AA and the evolution of the Twelve Steps? Bill Wilson, months before he met up with the Oxford Group, had read and reread Mary Baker Eddy's *Science and Health with Key to the Scriptures* in the hope of overcoming his drinking by strengthening his willpower.[5] Though this did not work, Bill and his associate Hank P. probably had Mrs. Eddy's book in mind when they later developed the text *Alcoholics Anonymous*.[6] At a still later time, Bill Wilson became convinced, through his reading, that Mrs. Eddy had not given due credit for initial help she had received from Phineas Park Quimby. This had then created a long-running controversy which, Bill believed, could have been avoided if she had simply acknowledged Quimby's role.

Quimby, a self-educated clockmaker from Portland, Maine, is generally acknowledged as the founder of New Thought, which includes Unity, Divine Science, Religious Science and numerous related teachings. Although these organizations are outside mainstream Christianity, their literature has had considerable influence throughout American society.

William James had found answers to his own depression and doubts about his self-worth from the French philosopher Charles Bernard Renouvier and New Thought teachings, which he termed *mind-cure* in his chapter titled "The Religion of Healthy-Mindedness."[7] In the same section, he quoted Ralph Waldo Trine's *In Tune with the Infinite,* a famous New Thought book first published in 1897 that has been almost continuously in print.[8]

While New Thought organizations never became very large, their ideas have had wide acceptance in general society and also influenced AA. Early AA members, according to Nell Wing, were urged to read James Allen's *As a Man Thinketh,* Thomas Troward's *Edinburgh Lectures on Mental Science,* and Emmet Fox's *The Sermon on the Mount.* Mike E., the second AA member from Detroit, often mentioned the inspiration he received from Fox's book when he started his recovery in 1938, even before the publication of *Alcoholics Anonymous.*

What did these New Thought books offer that had already influenced American society and would also benefit the early AA members?

The principal benefit of New Thought was much like the program of the Oxford Group and the claims of William James in his seminal book. It transformed religious beliefs into a plan of action that individuals could follow for their own benefit in solving problems *here and now.* Charles S. Braden, a religious historian, said that most of what was included in New Thought was not new at all. "Almost all of its major ideas had appeared at some period in the history of the Christian faith, or, if not there, certainly in some of the other religions of the world," he said. Its basic belief, he added, could be traced certainly as far back as Plato.[9]

One important idea of New Thought was about the

accessibility and availability of God, or Higher Power. This Higher Power is often described in New Thought teachings as an All Powerful, Guiding, Creative Intelligence—a term that also appears in the text *Alcoholics Anonymous* (p. 49). Also paramount in New Thought is the term *consciousness*, which describes what one is thinking and feeling at all levels. *Alcoholics Anonymous* (p. 51) uses the term in this way: "When many hundreds of people are able to say that the consciousness of the Presence of God is today the most important fact of their lives, they present a powerful reason why one should have faith." The Presence of God, an idea closely identified with the great Catholic mystic Brother Lawrence, is a key point in New Thought; indeed, the Divine Science branch of New Thought emphasizes this as "Omnipresence." And whereas the AA text refers to this as a "great fact," Ralph Waldo Trine had pretty much the same idea in 1897 when he wrote: "The great central fact in human life, in your life and in mine, is the coming into a conscious, vital realization of our oneness with this Infinite Life, and the opening of ourselves fully to this divine flow."[10]

The book *Alcoholics Anonymous* also describes the experience of an alcoholic who "was overwhelmed by a conviction of the Presence of God. . . . He stood in the Presence of Infinite Power and Love. . . . For the first time, he lived in conscious companionship with his Creator" (p. 56). This language, though it would be acceptable to most Christian religions, is more often found in New Thought circles.

There are some grounds for believing, too, that the term *conscious contact*, which appears in AA's Step Eleven, may have emerged from the lectures of Emmet Fox in New York City, which Bill and Lois Wilson attended with other AA members in the late 1930s. Though it is a fairly ordinary term, it was probably used by Fox in lectures in the months just before Bill Wilson wrote the Twelve Steps.[11]

Both the Oxford Group and New Thought emphasized "seeking Divine Guidance" and the importance of keeping one's thinking straight—eliminating hateful, resentful thoughts and seeking to maintain warm, forgiving attitudes toward everybody. The New Thought groups, however, attach more importance to finding physical healing and attaining personal success, while Buchman and the Oxford Group seemed more attuned to the task of healing society and patching up one's troubled relationships with others. Important to both groups, however, was the belief that one's *thinking* eventually produces corresponding outcomes in one's life.

Since Bill Wilson and the AA pioneers realized from the beginning that they wanted to focus on the single purpose of helping alcoholics, they had little to say about seeking physical healings or achieving success in one's work. They had a lot to say, however, about the role of one's *thinking* in finding and maintaining sobriety. AA members have freely admitted that "stinking thinking" has a lot to do with one's "stinking drinking," an idea that agrees with the New Thought idea that bad thinking brings bad results. The AA practice of taking inventory and working on personal shortcomings and similar practices involve cleaning up one's thinking, which thereby brings improvements in one's life.

Though it was not looked upon as a "spiritual" program, the Coué movement, popular in the 1920s, may have helped prepare the way for the general acceptance of self-help methods and even the ideas of Freud, Adler, and Jung. This was the view of Dr. Leslie D. Weatherhead, a prominent British minister and author who made a definitive study of spiritual healing movements.

One of the lasting ideas of the Coué movement was the power of *suggestion* and the possibility of improving one's self with *autosuggestion.* Emile Coué (1857-1926) was a pharmacist in Nancy, France, who became interested in the use of hypnosis in treating physical ailments. Along the way, he became convinced that people had within themselves the power to change their lives and heal distressed conditions simply by repeating the helpful phrase, "Every day in every way I am getting better and better." Still followed by many people today, and closely related to New Thought and positive thinking, the Coué system had great success. According to Weatherhead, it swept across Europe "like a prairie fire" and drew more than a hundred patients a day to Coué's modest home in Nancy. The method, and Coué's self-improvement slogan, became a stock phrase almost overnight, one magazine reported in November 1922,[12] and Coué himself became the subject of sensational press coverage when he embarked on an American lecture tour early the following year. In America, as in Europe, dramatic healings and other beneficial results were claimed and reported.

Though it eventually came to be seen as a passing fad, Coué's popular psychology had some lasting effects. "To the minds of ordinary people," Weatherhead wrote, "Coué brought home a most important truth: the power of the mind over the body."[13] Couéism also helped publicize a related truth that is important in recovery for alcoholics. This is the apparent supremacy of the human imagination in any contest with the human will. C. Harry Brooks, a Coué student, described it thus: "This explains the baffling experience of the drug-taker, the drunkard, the victim of some vicious craving. His mind is obsessed by the desire for satisfaction. The efforts of the will to restrain it only make it more overmastering. Repeated failures convince him at length that he is powerless to control himself, and this idea, operating as an autosuggestion, increases his impotence. So in despair, he abandons himself to his obsession, and his life ends in wreckage."[14]

According to Emile Coué, such an outcome was the logical result of the Law of Reversed Effort: "When the will and imagination are in conflict, the imagination invariably gains the day." Translated to the world of alcoholism, this simply means that the alcoholic is usually his own worst enemy when he seeks to marshal his willpower to keep from drinking. The imagination intrudes by raising delightful pictures that intensify even as the alcoholic seeks to suppress them. Finally the tension becomes unbearable, and he is carried back to the bottle as if led by a powerful but invisible hand.

What did AA give the alcoholic as a defense in this unequal contest with the imagination? First, it recognized that the will is of little use in directly combatting the obsession to drink. Second, AA uses the imagination in constructive ways by creating pictures of the benefits sobriety can bring. The third and most important defense supplied by AA is the belief in a Higher Power, active and benign in one's life.

Coué did not present his teachings in quite the same way; Higher Power, to him, was apparently the individual's own, powerful subconscious mind. But Coué himself was a friendly, loving man of high moral character. He had strong religious beliefs and even his critics acknowledged that he exemplified Christian principles in his life. Brooks, a devoted Coué disciple, wrote that Coué's method "teaches the doctrine of the inner life which saints and sages have proclaimed through all ages. It asserts that within are the sources of calm, of power and courage, and that the man who has once attained mastery of this inner sphere is secure in the face of all that may befall him." Brooks went on to suggest that the affirmation in Coué's formula was a kind of prayer, and he asked, "Does it not appeal to something beyond the self-life, to the infinite power lying behind us?"[15]

In his 1923 American tour, Coué also realized—as his fellow countryman Tocqueville had nearly one hundred years earlier—that Americans were intensely interested in the practical side of any teaching. According to Richard Huber, Coué observed that the French were content to argue on the fundamentals of principle. "The American mind, on the other hand, is teeming with plans to put the principle to work, 'to carry the idea further even than the author of it may have conceived,' and to discover 'its practical adaptability to everyday life.' "[16]

This had the inevitable result of causing Couéism to be seen as a fast route to business success, which brought about criticism and disillusionment. Like most faith or mental healing movements, it also became controversial as a means of overcoming illness and disease. Some viewed it as both selfish and self-centered, or simply another cunning scheme for getting one's way in the world. By the end of the 1920s and following Coué's death, the method came to be seen as a passing fad, though its affirmation has endured.

If Couéism made any contribution to AA, it was in presenting a strong case for the self-help that lies within any individual's reach. In very simple terms, Coué explained that people are defeated by the same thought powers which can also bring about their liberation when properly employed. It cleared the way for a general acceptance of our own responsibility for facing the inner demons that have been driving us to destruction.

Another event in the same time period that had some bearing on AA's spiritual development was the publication of Bruce Barton's *The Man Nobody Knows* in 1925. Although this book is nowhere to be found in AA group libraries today, it was still included on a list of recommended books for AA members circulated in California in 1948. Its value to the early AA society may have been in presenting the *human* side of Jesus rather than the other-worldly concept that may have been so intimidating for many people.

Barton was one of America's most successful advertising executives, and his book made some critics squirm at the same time it climbed to the top of the best-seller lists. Richard M. Huber noted, with great scorn, that Barton did not begin with the "typical" businessman and relate him to Christ. Rather, Barton reversed the process and showed how Christ was eminently qualified as a businessman. Jesus was portrayed as a great executive who knew how to pick and train men, an outdoorsman, and "the most popular dinner guest in Jerusalem." Moreover, Jesus was not the weak, ascetic person shown in many illustrations; instead, he had an outflow of health that healed others and a personality that appealed to women (because women like strength). He also knew the value of advertising!

Since a large part of Barton's message was on business success and how Jesus fitted in with the American dream of such
success, his book came in for sharp criticism. It has even been
lumped with Couéism as a symbol of the Roaring Twenties,
when it appeared to some that the sensational business expansion would go on forever and was the Will of God. Intellec-
tuals hated his book, which was rejected by the distinguished
Maxwell Perkins of Scribner before finally landing with Bobbs-
Merrill in Indianapolis, also the publishers of Trine's *In Tune
with the Infinite.* This intellectual aversion to Barton's book must
have also been shared by many alcoholics who were probably
surprised to find it as recommended AA reading.

The book made the list, however, because of the very real
AA need to bring religious truth into practical human affairs.
Even if most books of this genre were employed to justify or
promote business success, AA had an ability to use the same
ideas for its own primary purpose: success in staying sober,
success in practicing the Twelve Step principles. While this also
brought business recovery or success for many AA members,
such success has never been considered the primary reason
for following the AA program.

Far more important than Barton to AA was Emmet Fox,
whose 1934 book *The Sermon on the Mount* became one of the
society's most useful guides until the publication of *Alcoholics
Anonymous* in 1939. Bill Wilson freely acknowledged the importance of the book to AA, though insisting that it was not
needed after the Big Book was published. He also said that
he and other early AA members attended Fox's lectures in New
York City in the late 1930s. *The Sermon on the Mount* was offered for sale by many AA groups. (It is sometimes excluded
today by groups whose policy is to stock only AA Conference-
approved publications.)

While the jacket calls it "The Key to Success in Life," Fox's
book contains little of the brimming praise for American
business that Barton exuded. But like Barton, Fox took Jesus'
teachings in *The Sermon on the Mount* and showed how they

could be applied in one's life to solve practical problems. Even though the book hardly mentions alcoholism, it carries a message that many recovering people have found vital and useful.

There was also a great difference in the social climate that faced each message upon publication. *The Man Nobody Knows* was published in the business boom of the 1920s; Fox's book was released during one of the worst years of the Great American Depression. It was first offered, in fact, in the same year Bill Wilson was bottoming out to begin the painful trek to sobriety and recovery. Fox was said to have a strong appeal to the business community, but his ministry usually focused on inspiring people who were beaten and discouraged, not in cheering successful people on to further achievements.

For the alcoholic, one of Fox's main points was the need to forgive others and "let them go." He warned again and again of the danger *to oneself* of holding grudges and resentments, or in trying to seek revenge. He was also strong in asserting that "prayer changes things" and that "thoughts become part of one's future experience." As for the miracles presented in the Bible, he argued that they occurred and were not a violation of natural law but simply a manifestation of higher laws.

Fox never had any direct connection with AA, other than through his books, but his ministry seemed to have been timed to be of considerable benefit to the shaping of the fellowship. Born in Ireland in 1886, he grew up in England and became an electrical engineer (the same profession that had attracted Bill Wilson in college). Ill health and other personal problems drove him to seek possible answers in New Thought teachings, particularly the writings of Thomas Troward, a former British judge in India whose Edinburgh lectures established him as a prominent early New Thought writer. According to an associate, Fox found his first New Thought books while browsing in a used-book shop in London. Gaining victory over his health problems and acquiring both confidence and speaking power, he became a lecturer in England in the late 1920s.

In 1931, Fox came to New York on a six-month visa to lecture at various New Thought groups. He arrived just when the Church of the Healing Christ, a Divine Science church, was seeking a new pastor. Invited to speak as a guest, he immediately attracted huge audiences. He was then offered a permanent post with the church, where he remained until his death in 1951. Always popular, he spoke to as many as four thousand in sessions at the old Hippodrome theater. He held regular services at Carnegie Hall in later years, often attended by a thousand or more. His books have continued to be published by Harper & Row, now HarperCollins.

Fox's influence on society and AA has been something of a puzzle. He was called a cultist by some, though he was by all accounts a conservative, proper man who would have seemed at home in the pastorate of a mainstream church. Norman Vincent Peale, whose own ministry was just beginning at New York's Marble Collegiate Church, deplored the popular psychology in Fox's teachings and sought to offer an alternative. Later on, however, Peale himself would come under attack for offering "pop psychology" rather than what his critics viewed as true religion.

The key to Fox's appeal, however, lay in his strong personal belief in his teachings and his ability to offer practical ways of using spiritual methods—particularly prayer and meditation—to solve personal problems. Like the Oxford Group, Fox's students learned to practice daily prayer and to seek guidance on matters of concern. Charles S. Braden, noting that Fox's influence went far beyond New Thought circles, offered this comment: "[Fox] was in no way sensational either in his language, in his ideas, or in his illustrations. Compared to such performances as those of Aimee Semple McPherson, Billy Sunday, or even Billy Graham, his services were models of quiet, thoughtful, prayerful worship. He was very down-to-earth. He made things as simple as profound truth can be made. He was direct. He was forthright. He had a warmth about him that drew people to him personally, though he was not gregarious and had few close friends or associates. But he was deeply sincere. He was hopeful. He was optimistic in the best sense, and so utterly sure of the gospel and its workability that his quiet confidence led men to want to hear him. His message was for 'right now.' He had a faith in the future—of that no one can doubt who reads him—but his religion was for here and now—and people needed just that."[17]

It was this "here and now" element in Fox's messages that also must have appealed to the AA pioneers. *The Sermon on the Mount* was popular with Dr. Bob Smith and the early Akron members, and is still offered for sale by some groups in the Midwest.[18]

Another surprising self-help development in the mid-1930s was the appearance of the runaway best-seller, *How to Win Friends and Influence People,* by Dale Carnegie. Though this had no connection with the budding AA fellowship when released in 1936, it expressed the self-help philosophy in American society. One of the all-time best-sellers, this book and Carnegie have often been criticized, frequently by the same people who found fault with Couéism, Bruce Barton, and others. But thousands, including Soviet President Mikhail Gorbachev, have acknowledged a debt to Carnegie, whose writings—when studied fairly—are highly compatible with AA principles. And not incidentally, Bill Wilson and some of his early Oxford Group associates took the Dale Carnegie speaking course in New York City.

One Carnegie idea, appearing in 1936, may have found its way, three years later, as AA's Tenth Step, which suggests continuing to take inventory and promptly admitting it when wrong. Carnegie phrased it this way: "When we are wrong—and that will be surprisingly often, if we are honest with ourselves—let's admit our mistakes quickly and with enthusiasm."[19]

Carnegie also had much to say about sincerity, withholding criticism, and expressing encouragement to others—all important ideas in AA. He emphasized the necessity of giving advice *indirectly*—that is, by suggestion—rather than imposing one's own views on the other person. Though this has been condemned as manipulative since it is designed to aid one's own business success, it is exactly what AA members are urged to do in their own presentation of the program to others.

Despite all the ideas gleaned from various sources, however, AA itself was still a new idea when it finally emerged as a separate society in the 1938-1939 period. Whatever it owed to the mutual self-help ideas that were in the general atmosphere, the AA society was still a new creation with a distinct character of its own. Bill Wilson's great achievement was in shaping the AA program, struggling hard to keep the infant society working in unity, and then guiding it through the trial period as it grew into an institution that has effectively aided millions in recovery.

It's not surprising that Wilson found useful a number of ideas that were related to business. Though his early career as a stockbroker had been blunted by alcoholism and bad luck, he was actually a gifted business analyst whom one market titan—the late Joe Hirschhorn—considered the best on Wall Street. Wilson's work in forming AA was much like the work of an entrepreneur in putting together a budding business enterprise. Moreover, Wilson often used such business terms as *inventory* and *liabilities* to relate to alcoholism and recovery.

Another aspect of Wilson's personality was *practicality.* Though he was a sensitive, idealistic man, he was chiefly interested in ideas that *worked,* or showed some promise of working in the future. When he borrowed ideas from anybody, whether it was the Oxford Group or William James or Emmet Fox, he was always selective. He was careful not to become too closely identified with anything in the other teachings that might be harmful to AA.

Whatever its sources, the AA society has borne out what Tocqueville observed a hundred years before the fellowship was launched. It was created by people looking "for mutual assistance; and as soon as they. . .found each other out, they combine[d]. From that moment they [were] no longer isolated men, but a power seen from afar, whose actions serve for an example, and whose language is listened to."[20] And in its way, AA has conditioned the general atmosphere for the appearance of more self-help societies, many with the "Anonymous" tag!

CHAPTER EIGHT

Richard Peabody and The Emmanuel Movement: An Early Breakthrough in Boston

One of the most intriguing coincidences in AA history—although it's never mentioned—is that Bill and Lois Wilson attended Calvary Church Oxford Group meetings while a recovering alcoholic named Richard Peabody was treating clients at his home less than a block away, at 24 Gramercy Park.

This was an important New York City connection for early AA understanding, but it actually had a Boston beginning under religious auspices. Peabody, who died in 1936, is best remembered today for his book, *The Common Sense of Drinking,* which included important articles printed in medical journals in 1930 and 1931. Though he was a nonprofessional who came to be known as a "lay therapist," Peabody helped educate his generation of medical doctors about the hopelessness of the alcoholic's condition. He also won a very modest acceptance of lay therapists as co-workers with psychiatrists in treating alcoholics. He trained other recovering alcoholics to carry on the same work, and one of his best-known protégés was lay therapist Francis T. Chambers, Jr., who worked in Philadelphia with Dr. E. A. Strecker.[1]

Peabody's contribution to AA has to be inferred from his writing and the coincidental events that accompanied his work.

But since *The Common Sense of Drinking* preceded the AA Big Book by some years and was one of the most highly regarded early books about alcoholism, it's believed that Bill Wilson consulted it as he set about writing his own material. It is startling, for example, to find in Peabody's writing some of the phrases and ideas that have become part of AA. "Halfway measures are of no avail," Peabody wrote, in discussing what the alcoholic must do to recover.[2] Did Bill Wilson use this same idea when he said, "Half measures availed us nothing" in the famous Chapter Five passage that now serves as an introduction to AA meetings?

Peabody also put forth the idea that complete surrender had to precede getting sober: "The surrender to the fact that alcohol can no longer be indulged in without bringing disastrous results is of such importance that it requires extremely thoughtful consideration" (p. 74). He deplored the "going-on-the-wagon point of view" as only a stopgap measure, and referred to failed attempts to teach alcoholics "to drink like gentlemen" (p. 81). He emphasized the need for honesty. "Once the alcoholic takes up treatment," he wrote, "he must be absolutely honest in giving an account of his thoughts and actions, and he must take great precautions against lying ingeniously (rationalizing) to himself." Quoting another source, Peabody affirmed that frankness and honesty were a first principle of mental hygiene (p. 97).

Peabody also briefly mentioned (p. 123) an unknown man who gave up drinking until he had made his fortune five years later. Resuming "moderate" drinking, he was soon back in his alcoholic difficulties, losing his money in two or three years and dying of alcoholism a few years after that. This anecdotal account may have been the germ idea for the Big Book story (pp. 32-33) about the "man of thirty" who gave up drinking until successful retirement at fifty-five, and then picked up the bottle again, with disastrous results.

Though this undoubtedly happened to a number of alcoholics, it's not hard to believe that Peabody's simple anecdote was enlarged for greater effect as Bill Wilson developed it. An alternate explanation is that another alcoholic embroidered Peabody's story and then passed it on to Wilson in the much more dramatic form that appears in the Big Book. If Wilson did improve on the story, he can be forgiven this slight enhancement when it's remembered that he was fighting desperately against great odds to build a strong case for sobriety. Wilson was using every tool he could find, because even the one hundred recoveries AA claimed by early 1939 included some who were very shaky and later returned to drinking.

Like the people who contributed medical knowledge to AA, Peabody suspected that alcoholism was partly produced by an inborn cause. This idea was similar to the "allergy" suggested by Dr. William D. Silkworth in his comments for the AA Big Book. Peabody thought the alcoholic inherits "a nervous system which is non-resistant to alcohol." While the use of the term "allergy" is today rejected by professionals, there is now growing acceptance of the belief that genetic factors are involved in alcoholism. But Silkworth must have been influenced by Peabody's writings, as other doctors were. Peabody and Silkworth at least had the same idea: that something beyond the control of alcoholics predisposed them to their drinking problem.

Though most of Peabody's ideas and principles seem elementary today, they were extremely important in his day. For one thing, drunkenness was still widely seen as a moral issue, and the United States had embarked on an ill-starred flirtation with national Prohibition in an effort to solve the problem. But it was also believed by many—as it still is by some today—that alcoholics were simply weak and irresponsible, and by using better judgment could have "trained" themselves to be controlled drinkers. Finally, another theory, this one growing out of the psychiatric profession and Freudian thinking, was that extensive psychoanalysis could remove alcoholics' reasons for drinking, thereby changing them either into controlled drinkers or well-adjusted abstainers. Peabody's book, and his professional work, helped to discredit such views, thus paving the way for a more effective approach.

But Peabody did not, as has been suggested, set forth all the principles of AA. Though he advocated many ideas about alcoholism and recovery that now parallel those in AA, he failed to sufficiently target the extreme dangers of the resentment, fear, and self-pity that plague many alcoholics in sobriety. Some of his clients did become lay therapists working in alcoholism; yet, Peabody had no real group support system to sustain the alcoholic.

The most glaring deficiency in his program, at least in terms of AA thinking, was its lack of spiritual content. And this deficiency was difficult to explain, because Peabody himself had recovered in the Boston Emmanuel Movement, a powerful spiritual program operating under a unit of the Episcopal church. Like New Thought and Christian Science, the Emmanuel Movement had been cited approvingly by William James in *The Varieties of Religious Experience.*

The movement itself was started in the 1905-1906 period at Boston's Emmanuel Church by a minister, Dr. Elwood Worcester, with the assistance of a colleague, Dr. Samuel McComb. One of their early motives was somewhat competitive. As members of the mainstream Episcopal church, they had watched with some dismay the astonishing growth of Christian Science, which was headquartered in Boston. With the Emmanuel Movement, Worcester sought to prove that the same healing powers and other benefits that Christian Science promised could also be generated by an established Christian church.

Writing in the *North American Review* of March 1909, Dr. Samuel McComb discussed the background for the establishment of Emmanuel clinic. It had begun with the startling idea of holding a "tuberculosis class" to help poor people afflicted with consumption while allowing them to remain in their homes. A doctor supervised the effort—unlike Christian Scientists, Worcester and McComb took great care to include medical doctors in their work. "The treatment offered consisted of the most recent scientific method of combating consumption," McComb wrote, "along with the psychic forces of discipline, friendly encouragement, hope and material help—in short, a combination of physical, psychical and moral elements. This effort has been attended with the most gratifying success, and it is being followed in other places," he added. He noted, too, that the work had been commended by Professor William Osler (who was then one of the world's most distinguished medical educators).

The success of the tuberculosis class then led them, McComb said, to bring medicine and clergy together in helping "the morally and nervously disordered." This soon included a number of alcoholics, although this group was apparently never more than 12 percent of the troubled people helped at the clinic.

Dr. Katherine McCarthy, a professor of sociology at Southern Connecticut State University, has written scholarly papers about Worcester's method of healing for these assorted forms of "nervousness," including alcoholism and other addictions. Their free clinic was widely publicized during its twenty-three years of operation, McCarthy said, and Worcester and McComb became well known for their success with alcoholics as well as other types of patients.[3] After 1929, Worcester carried on his work under the title "The Craigie Foundation."

A leading British clergyman, Dr. Leslie D. Weatherhead, who wrote extensively on psychology and religion until his death in 1976, gave Worcester considerable credit for recognizing the value of both medicine and religion in the cure of body, mind, and spirit, and for using both in the art of healing.[4] In its ability to adapt from both fields, the Emmanuel Movement was very close to the ideal expressed by Bill Wilson, who always acknowledged the contributions to AA made by medicine and religion. Psychotherapy alone, according to Worcester, was mere patchwork without "the renewal of life at its source and its regulation by spiritual principles and laws." Worcester claimed superior results for the Emmanuel clinic's methods, which were also supported by a prominent psychiatrist and author, Dr. Isador H. Coriat.

Though it failed to displace either Christian Science or New Thought, the Emmanuel Movement achieved remarkable success and served as a model for similar church-related clinics later on. It has to be considered a forerunner of the soon-to-be-acceptable "mind and body" school of medicine, which increasingly focused on emotional and mental causes of physical ailments. The movement also made a good beginning in helping alcoholics. Worcester and his colleagues had a number of beliefs that would still be considered sound today: they insisted, for example, that alcoholics had to abstain from even one drink in order to recover; they did not moralize, scold, or preach temperance; and they believed in the power of prayer and meditation. Moreover, they were kindly, warm-hearted people with a sincere desire to help others.

In 1913, according to McCarthy, a man named Courtenay Baylor joined the movement as a specialist in alcoholism; she even suggests that Baylor may have been the first paid alcoholism therapist in this country.[5] Baylor, a problem drinker himself, had found help two years earlier at the church. He went on to have a fairly successful career as an alcoholism therapist, and also wrote a book titled *Remaking a Man* in 1919. One of his patients was Richard Peabody, who later dedicated *The Common Sense of Drinking* to Baylor.

Peabody had started visiting the Emmanuel clinic in 1922, following a stormy drinking career that had left his life in ruins. Much of what is known about Richard Peabody's drinking comes from accounts by or about his first wife, Polly, who later changed her name to "Caresse" after divorcing Peabody and marrying an alcoholic named Harry Crosby. (And, continuing a pattern that is recognized today as common among spouses of alcoholics, Caresse married another alcoholic after Crosby's suicide in 1929.)

Peabody, though a few years older than Bill Wilson, grew

up and acquired bad drinking habits in the same time setting that brought the AA co-founder to the brink of destruction. Unlike Wilson, who felt some early inferiority about his family background and education, Peabody had the advantage of Groton boarding school training and college at Harvard. He was a member of one of Massachusetts's most distinguished families and also a godson of J. P. Morgan. Like Wilson, he took military training at Plattsburg and served in France as a commissioned officer during World War I. He married Polly in 1915, and years later, in an autobiography of her chaotic but interesting life, she wrote about the experience of joining his family of Boston Brahmins.

Peabody apparently had little talent for business or was sidetracked by his drinking, because he soon lost their money in a shipping-business venture. They had two children, but by the early 1920s Polly had left him for Crosby. Polly wrote that though he was shattered by the divorce, it was evidently a factor in his search for recovery. With the help of Charles Codman, a close friend, Peabody was put in touch with Worcester and Emmanuel clinic, according to Polly. "Little by little he joined in the work and he, too, began to talk with and influence his contemporaries whose weakness for alcohol had been their undoing," she said. "This work took on more and more importance, and he himself effected some remarkable cures. He even came to be spoken of as 'Dr.' Peabody, and though he was self-taught and a layman, he decided to set up an informal office in Newbury Street [in Boston].... His advice was, 'When you need a drink you need a friend. Come to me then, we will talk it out at any time, day or night.' He was a fore-runner of the famous Alcoholics Anonymous."[6]

Katherine McCarthy believes that Peabody received referrals from Courtenay Baylor, though by 1933 he had transferred his practice to New York. Baylor, she says, believed that alcoholism resulted from mental and physical "tenseness," so he followed Worcester's lead in using a relaxation therapy. Peabody also favored relaxation techniques, and he even had his patients develop and follow detailed time plans for each day.

In summarizing his recovery program, Peabody expressed beliefs that reflected the teachings of both Coué and New Thought. Paralleling Coué's view on the power of suggestion, he wrote: "The unconscious mind can be influenced by suggestion so that it cooperates with the conscious to bring about a consistent, intelligent course of action." And as both Coué and New Thought teachers would have said, he went on to note that actions "are the direct result of thoughts. Experience has proved over and over again that thoughts can be definitely controlled and directed when it seems desirable to do so."[7]

Peabody, in stating such views, was only a step away from the belief in Higher Power that was well entrenched in New England. Katherine McCarthy also noted that the roots of the Peabody Method were in Protestant religious thought and were based on Elwood Worcester's beliefs about the interrelationship of body, mind, and spirit. Even though Worcester's work was religious and/or spiritual in content, Peabody and his followers made serious compromises in it in the hope, she said, that they could be accepted as having some of the same authority as psychiatrists. McCarthy noted, however, that this hope was unfulfilled. She added, "Peabody and his followers essentially gutted their method of the vital substance that had made Worcester and Baylor so successful in earlier decades."[8]

But it's also possible that Peabody—like many AA members—never really bought into the spiritual program offered by his sponsors. His writings suggest that self-knowledge, retraining, discipline, and cultivation of new habits were enough to establish sobriety and maintain it. And though he called for "surrender," this was merely the surrender of the belief that one could someday drink safely. Peabody did not mention a spiritual surrender of the type Bill Wilson described in his own experience. Peabody's work added to the knowledge of alcoholic treatment and helped promote what became known as the "disease concept," but he did not advocate a spiritual program in spite of having benefited from spiritually minded mentors.

Courtenay Baylor, however, was still living in Boston when AA became rooted there, and early members remembered him. Faye R., according to Katherine McCarthy, said that Baylor attended an AA meeting, loved it, and enthusiastically recommended it to her. McCarthy also pointed out, in 1984, that Emmanuel Church now housed an AA meeting; "it meets on Wednesdays in the old parish house, the same place where Worcester and McComb gave Wednesday night classes for up to a thousand 'nervous sufferers.' "

While the religious program of the Emmanuel Movement had no direct funnel into AA, it did pave the way for joint efforts by clergy and medicine in working with troubled people. Since it was also sponsored by an Episcopal church, its example must have influenced Sam Shoemaker in New York and others who tried to apply Christian principles to mental health problems. And its great additional benefit was in aiding Richard Peabody to recovery, whose work certainly laid part of the foundation for AA.

Despite its early promise, the Peabody Method's one-on-one approach probably did not survive beyond the 1950s.[9] Faye R., the longtime AA member interviewed by Katherine McCarthy, was a patient of Baylor and two Peabody-Method therapists during her beginning efforts to find sobriety.

But Faye's success came only when she found AA. Her observation just about says it all: "They [the Peabody therapists] had many wonderful ideas but they just didn't have the magic of AA."

CHAPTER NINE

AA's Roots in The Old-Time Religion

Ebby T., when he carried the Oxford Group message to Bill Wilson in late 1934, was living in a mission that virtually practiced what could be called "The Old-Time Religion." Calvary Mission, even with the sponsorship of a modern Episcopal church, had the atmosphere and many of the practices of a Gospel revival organization. Along with hymn singing, this included an altar call as a climax to the religious services. The altar call, still common today in evangelical revivals, has been sneeringly referred to on skid row as "taking a nose dive."

Some AA members were outspoken in their resistance to this kind of religious practice. One early AA member recalled his bitterness that, as a young boy, he was forced to "come forward and accept Jesus or face a razor strap behind the barn." And there has always been a studied effort in AA to avoid any terms or practices that would tie the fellowship to a specific type of religion.

But AA's spiritual roots may reach more deeply into "The Old-Time Religion" than many AA members would suspect. Just as the fellowship owes a debt to Frank Buchman and the Oxford Group, so did it also receive some of its force from the work of evangelically based leaders of the nineteenth and early twentieth centuries. These leaders either influenced Buchman and his associates or set in motion ideas that were of benefit to AA. They are never mentioned in AA writings, but Jerry McAuley, General William Booth, Charles G. Finney, and Dwight L. Moody left their mark on society and religion in ways that eventually touched AA. Two others who also influenced the spiritual beginnings of AA were Robert E. Speer and Henry B. Wright.

Jerry McAuley:
A Mean Drunk Who Recovered
To Help Others

Harry Hadley, it was noted in Chapter Three, was the son of S. H. Hadley, who had run the famous Jerry McAuley Water Street Mission in New York City. It was this tradition that led to Harry Hadley's own conversion and burning desire to follow in his father's path by helping defeated men through mission work. Joining with Sam Shoemaker, Harry Hadley carved his own niche in setting up Calvary Mission, Ebby T.'s base as he set out to help Bill Wilson.

But if there was a pattern setter for this type of service, it was Jerry McAuley. Born in Ireland in 1839, McAuley came to New York at age thirteen and quickly became both a thief and a drunk. His thefts and assaults on others netted him short stays in the city prison, finally building up to a robbery charge that landed him in Sing Sing penitentiary with a fifteen-and-one-half-year sentence. McAuley was only nineteen, but he was, according to his biographer Arthur Bonner, "such a nuisance and terror that even the rum sellers wanted to get rid of him."[1]

McAuley was guilty of many crimes, but ironically, he was sent to prison for one he didn't commit. He spent his first years bitterly plotting to murder the man who had betrayed him, and feeling great inner rage over the conditions of his life. Sing Sing officials, in the nineteenth century, ran the prison with tight discipline that included severe beatings and other cruel punishments.

Some years into his sentence, however, McAuley underwent a transforming conversion experience. He was a changed man when he was released from prison after serving more than seven years of his sentence. He also realized that drinking had been a major part of his problem and that he needed to maintain sobriety.

But loneliness overtook him, and his faith began to waver. He also found little support from the community. And disaster came when he took a room over a "lager bier" saloon. According to Arthur Bonner, this was a new drink for the slums, imported by the wave of German immigrants, so new that it was still spelled as a German phrase. "McAuley had never heard of it," Bonner wrote. "He was told it was a harmless drink, wholesome and good like root beer."

"I drank it and then began my downfall," McAuley later reported. "My head got confused. The old appetite was awakened. From that time I drank it every day and it was not long before I went from that to stronger liquors. The night I stopped praying I shall never forget. I felt as wretched as I did the day I went to prison."[2]

All unknowingly, McAuley had blundered into what AA members would someday call a slip. He plunged into more crime and degradation and made several failed attempts to regain both his faith and his sobriety. He finally found both.

It took some time before McAuley's acquaintances believed in his sincerity, but by the early 1870s he was able to win support for a new idea that had come to him: a mission where desperate, homeless people could find new hope and companionship with others who were also trying to live a new life. His Water Street Mission became so successful in carrying out its aims that when McAuley died in 1884, his funeral was attended by New York's leading citizens. As Bonner said, "Jerry McAuley was unique. . . . He was the first person in the world to open the doors of a religious institution every night of the year specifically for the outcasts of society. He was the first to start what we now know as a rescue mission. He raised a beacon where men and women burdened with misery, broken down and shattered by debauchery and vice, homeless and hopeless, hungry, ragged, defiled and drunk, from the prison or from the gutter, were welcomed and made to feel that somebody cared for them. He showed them they could be saved in the spirit and made decent and respectable here and now in this life."[3]

For AA's future purposes, Jerry McAuley also contributed several important ideas. One may have been in his unfortunate slip through drinking "lager bier." This certainly would have convinced him and later mission workers that alcoholics cannot handle alcohol *in any form*. A second contribution was the conversion of S. H. Hadley, who ran the Water Street Mission after McAuley's death. Hadley served as an example for William James in *The Varieties of Religious Experience*, and also set a pattern for his own son to follow in opening Calvary Mission. Finally, Jerry McAuley proved, long before AA was started, that religious conversion can be a route to recovery for alcoholics.

General William Booth:
"Effectual Deliverance for the Drunkard"

Even as Jerry McAuley was launching his mission, spiritual help for alcoholics was reflected in the work of General William Booth and The Salvation Army in London. Booth was a Methodist minister at the beginning of his career, and he had the old-time preacher's attitude toward drinking. Yet he was one of the first religious leaders to suggest that alcoholism might be a disease, and he fought hard and successfully to help alcoholics recover. Booth lived elbow-to-elbow with the problem of alcoholism, and his wife, Catherine, his devoted partner in launching The Salvation Army, had grown up in an alcoholic home. (In the parlance of a current popular Twelve Step group, Catherine would now be called an "adult child.")

In 1890, the year of Catherine's death, General Booth released a tract titled *In Darkest England and the Way Out*. This publication, with part of its title—"The Way Out"—being the same as what AA almost selected as the title for its basic text, outlined the fiery General's prescriptions for social improvement. In a chapter titled "Effectual Deliverance for the Drunkard," Booth clearly showed his deep understanding of the compulsion to drink. Noting that many of their own Salvation Army workers were people who had been "abject slaves of the intoxicating cup," General Booth quickly conceded that those rescued were comparatively few of the huge number still in bondage. "The great reason for this is the simple fact that the vast majority of those addicted to the cup are its veritable slaves," he wrote. "No amount of reasoning, or earthly or religious considerations, can have any effect upon a man who is so completely under the mastery of this passion that he cannot break away from it, although he sees the most terrible consequences staring him in the face."

The General gave several accounts of alcoholics who had drunk themselves into hopelessness and then recovered through Salvation Army conversion. He also went on to suggest that types of homes be established to help persons who were attempting to recover. "While in one case drunkenness may be resolved into a habit, in another it must be accounted a disease," he wrote. "What is wanted in the one case, therefore, is some method of removing the man out of the sphere of the temptation, and in the other for treating the passion as a disease, as we should any other physical affliction, bringing to bear upon it every agency, hygienic and otherwise, calculated to effect a cure."[4]

By 1909, Booth and his followers had succeeded so well with alcoholics in London that a writer named Harold Begbie made this work the subject of a book titled *Twice-Born Men.*[5] This publication was, significantly, dedicated to William James, and it confirmed James's belief that religious experience can bring beneficial results in cases where people have been completely defeated.

There's little doubt that Frank Buchman and his early

followers were familiar with the message of *Twice-Born Men,*
especially since, in 1923, Begbie made Buchman and the Oxford
Group the subject of a sort of sequel, *More Twice-Born Men.*
And it's reasonable to believe that *Twice-Born Men* helped inspire Buchman in the Group's work with alcoholics in the 1920s
and early 1930s. Buchman always praised The Salvation Army
and endorsed its religious program, which he viewed as similar
to the Oxford Group's message. And it was mistakenly believed
by some that the woman minister who inspired Buchman's
change at Keswick in 1908 was Kate Booth-Clibborn, a daughter
of William Booth.[6]

Twice-Born Men, published by the Fleming H. Revell Company, was a huge publishing success that helped establish
Begbie's reputation as a religious writer. His book included personal accounts of London alcoholics who had found sobriety
and new happiness as a result of being converted by The Salvation Army. Somewhat like the AA Big Book thirty years
later, the stories about individuals carried descriptive names:
"A Copper Basher," "The Plumber," and "Lowest of the
Low." There was even one account—"The Puncher"—of an
alcoholic who later slipped and then came back to find successful recovery.

An important point in *Twice-Born Men* was that only the conversion experience—being "born again"—could have produced
the dramatic recoveries depicted in the book. Some of the subjects were criminal as well as alcoholic, and, as Begbie wrote,
"there is no medicine, no Act of Parliament, no moral treatise,
and no invention of philanthropy which can transform a man
radically bad into a man radically good." He argued that "only
religion can perform the miracle" needed to rescue masses of
people called hopeless and incurable. Noting that both science
and philanthropy had failed to solve the problem, he said, "It
is only religion that is not in despair about this mass of pro-
fitless evil dragging at the heels of progress—the religion which
still believes in miracle."

This point—"the religion which still believes in miracle"—

is an invisible bond that the present-day AA spiritual program shares with born-again movements and numerous cults and sects. Begbie, in writing about the degradation and hopelessness of the London disadvantaged, described conditions that are still prevalent today in most American cities. About the changes he had noted, he said, "If psychologists would know the secret of this miracle, working now in almost every country under the sun, they will find that it lies in using men once consciously wrong, inferior, and unhappy, using them to seek and to save, with a contagious joy and a vital affection, those of their own condition in life who are still consciously wrong, inferior, and unhappy. . . ."

Begbie also thought that the enthusiasm, joy, hymn-singing, and marching of The Salvation Army served important purposes in giving outcast and downtrodden people new goals and identity. He emphasized the need for strong feeling, and quoted Sir John Robert Seeley, a popular nineteenth century British historian and author, as a theme for his book: "No heart is pure that is not passionate; no virtue is safe that is not enthusiastic."[7]

AA, when it was formed, had no direct ties with Begbie, of course, and early AA members were always careful to distance their movement from anything that suggested reform or public conversion. Even as they rejected such ideas, however, they were benefiting from examples of recovery that evangelicals had brought about. Carl Jung and William James had both acknowledged religious experience as a possible answer to hopeless conditions. Books such as Begbie's showed how this worked in the practical world. Well in advance of the formation of AA, Begbie documented cases of hopelessness with spirit-based recoveries that were later repeated in AA with spectacular results.

Again, it should be emphasized that long before AA was established, it was proved and accepted that religious "conversion" or "change" was effective in overcoming alcoholism. AA's task was not to prove this, but to construct a method of change that would be acceptable to a larger number of alcoholics.

But William Booth and his Salvationists were not the only evangelicals to feed some of AA's early roots. Through the Oxford Group and Buchman's conversion experience, the fellowship also has links to the two great revivalists of nineteenth-century America, Charles G. Finney and Dwight L. Moody. Finney and Moody were the forerunners of modern revivalist movements similar to the Billy Graham ministry. Just as with the Oxford Group, their specific religious views and some of their jargon never carried over into AA. They did offer, however, religious belief that was strong with passion and enthusiasm, and they accepted both miracles and the importance of a conversion experience. Both men were also deeply concerned about the plight of problem drinkers and undoubtedly helped thousands find sobriety.

Charles Finney:
Evangelist and Reformer

Charles G. Finney, born in 1792, preceded Moody in the old-time revivalist tradition. Ernest Kurtz, author of the AA history *Not-God*, pointed out that Finney listed stages of "revival" that corresponded to the process that, 127 years later, Dr. Harry M. Tiebout would see as essential in the AA program. Finney framed the revival as "conviction of sin...a deep repentance, a breaking down of the heart...[and] reformation [of life]," Kurtz noted. Tiebout found similar stages, which he termed "hitting bottom, surrender, ego reduction, and maintenance of humility."[8] Neither Finney nor Tiebout might have been comfortable with this comparison, and yet they were not far apart in targeting the real needs of distressed human beings.

Finney, according to his biographers, initially wanted to study law and did not like the stern, orthodox Calvinism of his day. Noting that biblical references were included in many legal decisions, he started to read the scriptures and had a spontaneous religious "awakening." "He wanted to run his life as he pleased," Mark O. Guldseth wrote, "but he felt an ominous sense that a life of self-centeredness would bring him doom at its end. Early one morning, after a night of inner struggle, he was on the way to the office where he worked when he came to a clear understanding of what it meant for Jesus Christ to have given His life for him. So forceful was this realization that he stopped right in the middle of the road, apparently remaining there for several minutes. Later in the day he had further experiences convincing him of the love God had for him."[9]

This marked the beginning of an illustrious ministry that would have far-reaching influences on nineteenth-century America and is probably still influential today in ways that would be difficult to trace. Finney proved to be a masterful pulpit speaker, and he conducted revival campaigns in western New York, Philadelphia, Providence, and New York City. He addressed his audiences as sinners and prayed for them by name, as he carried his meetings out into the daylight of the streets where he sometimes even visited factories. Some church leaders and members balked at his approach, and it was noted that only his success at winning converts persuaded more orthodox clergymen to accept his views.

Finney attained additional distinction as an author, professor, and finally president of Oberlin College, which under his direction became known for its anti-slavery views and the educational opportunities it provided for many black students. Finney also promoted educational opportunities for women. He had many wealthy and influential supporters and won considerable backing for Oberlin College and philanthropic causes. In many ways, Finney had the social views of a modernist minister combined with the unshakable faith of the old-time preacher.

It was his religious influence that created spiritual ties to the early formation of AA. Mark Guldseth traced the effects of Finney's revivals in changing people who later did important work in England. The establishment of the famous Keswick religious conferences, where Buchman found his conversion, was a ripple effect from Finney's ministry. And in time, Finney's work reached Jessie Penn-Lewis, the woman who would profoundly change Buchman's life at Keswick in 1908.[10]

Dwight L. Moody:
The Northfield Conferences

Dwight L. Moody, undoubtedly the greatest evangelist of the last century, planted other spiritual roots which later influenced the Oxford Group and which survive in several changed forms in AA. Younger than Finney, Moody was born in 1837 in Northfield, Massachusetts, where he lived much of his life and died in the final month of the nineteenth century. Poorly educated in formal ways, he nonetheless founded three schools, including the Chicago Bible institute that bears his name. He is also credited with reshaping Victorian Christianity, despite the fact that he had no theological training.[11] And he is said to have carried his message to one hundred million people even without radio or television.

Moody, once a hustler and a born salesman, had become a successful shoe peddler in Chicago in his early years and was well on the way to starting a fortune. He had the energy and other qualities that would have made him a millionaire like his Chicago contemporary, the great retailing genius Marshall Field. But Moody's conversion in 1855 changed the direction of his life. He lost all interest in making money, and "winning souls for Christ" became his passionate objective.

By 1872, Moody was well on his way to world fame when he and his singing partner Ira Sankey went to Great Britain and launched a series of highly successful evangelical campaigns in Scotland and England. The campaigns attracted Henry Drummond, a professor at Edinburgh University and an author who attempted to harmonize the principles of Christianity with such issues as natural law and evolution. (Moody was deeply impressed by Drummond's talk, "The Greatest Thing in the World," and was largely responsible for its reaching a larger audience that would include pioneer AA members in the early 1930s and 1940s.) Moody and Drummond also became lifelong friends.

Returning to the United States, Moody then launched a series of revival campaigns in major cities. James Findlay, his biographer, wrote that Moody created the basic machinery of urban mass revivalism. "It was chiefly a feat of organization which sought to adapt the traditional theological and institutional practices of evangelical Protestantism to the new urban environment created by industrialism," Findlay said.[12]

In this changing new urban environment, alcoholism was also a problem of growing concern. The Washingtonians had disappeared, and the Wet/Dry controversy was coming into focus. Moody, though philosophically linked with the Drys, was only lukewarm toward Prohibition proposals. He was more interested in helping alcoholics through spiritual change, and there's little doubt that thousands did find sobriety in the conversion experience of the Moody revivals.

One reporter, for example, had come to the Moody meetings in a partly drunk condition, ribald and sneering. Some days later, Mark Guldseth writes, the reporter was seen again in a back seat. "I am waiting to thank Mr. Moody," he said. "I am a Christian, a new creature—not reformed, you can't reform a drunkard; I tried that a hundred times—but regenerated. I have reported sermons many a time, simply to ridicule them, but never had the least idea what true religion meant till I heard Mr. Moody ten days ago. . . . My children know the change [in me]; my wife knows it."[13]

But it was Moody's work at the Northfield, Massachusetts, student conferences that may have had the most lasting effect in presenting the ideas that were eventually funneled into AA. Moody founded two schools in his hometown, and one, the Northfield Seminary, became the site of the first Northfield summer student conference, in 1880. The Northfield conferences influenced an entire generation of ministers, including the individuals who would either have important roles in the Oxford Group or would contribute ideas to it. Both Frank Buchman and Sam Shoemaker, for example, were greatly inspired by their attendance at these immensely popular conferences.

Robert E. Speer:
Originator of the Four Absolutes

Cleveland AA members who visit their central office can still purchase a locally published booklet titled *The Four Absolutes.* This is a reminder of AA's Oxford Group origins. It reflects, additionally, the continuing interest in these standards that was shared by Dr. Bob and other early members in the Akron/Cleveland area. And though the Four Absolutes (Love, Honesty, Purity, and Unselfishness) were not included in the Big Book, Bill Wilson always insisted that such principles were represented in the Twelve Steps.

The Absolutes are an outgrowth of a Northfield conference and Dwight L. Moody's influence on Robert E. Speer, who presented them in a 1902 book, *The Principles of Jesus.*[14] Speer was a Princeton sophomore when he attended the Northfield Conference in 1887, the summer Henry Drummond delivered his soon-to-be-famous talk, "The Greatest Thing in the World." Even as a student, Speer felt the power and energy in Moody's personality, and he soon became a leader in subsequent conferences. Speer, after graduating from Princeton at the top of his class, became established as an important religious leader and author. Returning to the Northfield summer conferences as a speaker, he also influenced another Princeton student, Sam Shoemaker.

Henry B. Wright:
Proponent of Small Groups

Though Speer developed the argument for the Four Absolutes, these principles apparently came to Frank Buchman and the Oxford Group through Henry B. Wright, a highly acclaimed professor of religion at Yale. Wright's lecture room at Yale had these words from Dwight L. Moody on a wall: "The world has yet to see what God can do in, for, by and through a man whose will is wholly given up to Him." Wright reportedly started each lecture with a meditation on that idea, and then challenged his students to ask if any of them might become that person.

The determining factor in Wright's life and future career was a Northfield summer conference he attended immediately after his graduation from Yale in 1898. Moody, after addressing the students in an auditorium, called an additional meeting in another hall. Wright attended reluctantly, because he was afraid he might be asked to become a foreign missionary.

This did not happen, but he did become a missionary of another sort to hundreds of young men who studied under him, including Frank Buchman. Remembering Moody as "the greatest human I have ever known," Wright said that the evangelist sat in a large armchair at one end of the room, and "spoke to us simply and briefly about the issues of life, using John 7:17 as his theme: 'If any man willeth to do His will, he shall know of the teaching, whether it be of God, or whether I speak from myself.' There in the quiet, without any one knowing what was going on, I gave myself to God, my whole mind, heart, and body; and I meant it."[15]

In his teaching, Wright then became an unflinching advocate of the principles that would inspire Buchman and the Oxford Group: surrender, guidance, restitution, and witness. Wright and Buchman became good friends, worked together at the Northfield conferences, and exchanged ideas regularly. After Buchman joined Hartford Seminary, he even commuted

New Wine

to New Haven to attend Wright's lectures.

Wright, despite his gifts as a teacher, did not have a power-ful speaking voice. This kept him from reaching the large crowds that had flocked to hear Dwight L. Moody. But Wright formed small groups that proved to be highly effective in helping others to change. This may have given Buchman more confidence in the effectiveness of such groups and could have actually helped create the modern small-group movement exemplified by AA.

The Religious Climate that Followed Moody

It's doubtful that the three giants of nineteenth-century evangelism—General Booth, Charles Finney, and Dwight L. Moody—would be comfortable with the way the modern AA movement uses their principles and ideas. They might be hor-rified by the language at AA meetings, dismayed because Higher Power rather than Christ is the accepted AA term, and perplexed because AA limits its work mainly to helping drunks.

But they would certainly be in complete agreement with AA's single goal of helping alcoholics achieve sobriety. In their day as now, alcoholism was a great social evil that destroyed families and tore at the fabric of society. It's likely that General Booth looked upon drunkenness as the worst problem his organiza-tion had to face, and Moody, too, wept over the alcohol-induced suffering he saw in society.

Moody also worried about the fact that division in the Chris-tian denominations may have deflected efforts to help troubled people. In the last summer of his life, he explained that Chris-tian unity was the central idea of the Northfield Conference, though he also warned that this unity included "the Bible as it stands." He added, "We seek at these meetings to find points of common belief. Too frequently when Christians get together they seek for the points upon which they differ, and then go at it. The Christian denominations too often present a spec-tacle of a political party split into factions and unable to make an effective fight. Do you know that every twenty-four hours three hundred persons die a drunkard's death in this country? In the last four years there were thirty-eight thousand five hundred and twelve murders in this country. Here are things to unite on and combat."[16]

Unfortunately for Mr. Moody's dream, however, the Christian denominations were headed for even further dissension in the twentieth century. One great point of contention, for example, would be about "the Bible as it stands." Had they lived in a somewhat later time, Moody and devoted friends such as Drummond and Wright might have fallen out over this issue, as Christian fundamentalists and modernists did in the 1920s and beyond. Both General Booth and Dwight L. Moody were on the side of strict Bible believers, while Drummond and Wright showed signs of coming to terms with the scientific insights that had revolutionized modern society and cultural developments.

They did, however, share something that probably accounts for their great and lasting influence. This shared quality was a tremendous conviction of God's Love. This lit up their work and gave their sermons extraordinary power and purpose. Bonded in this Love, especially at the Northfield conferences, they had little time to quibble over the points that might have driven them apart. This Love, or compassion, is the great unifying spiritual quality that still works whenever it is really felt and put to work in human affairs. Maybe this is why Bill Wilson made AA unity a keystone of the fellowship's traditions.

CHAPTER TEN

AA's Boosters in The Modern Church

Writing AA's history for publication in 1957, Bill Wilson referred to the meeting twenty years earlier that led to John D. Rockefeller, Jr.'s, support of the fledgling movement.

One key person at this meeting in Rockefeller's boardroom was Albert Scott, chairman of trustees for Riverside Church and also president of Lockwood Greene Engineers, Inc., a prominent engineering firm. Listening to the accounts of recovery and release by Wilson and others, Scott exclaimed, "Why, this is first-century Christianity! What can we do to help?"[1]

Backed by Rockefeller, Scott and others provided enormous help in enlisting other nonalcoholic allies. They were able to convince Rockefeller to give just the right amount of financial support and assistance to the early movement. This became an important linkage in the fellowship's early success, leading to the writing and publication of *Alcoholics Anonymous* and the establishment of the Alcoholic Foundation.

But another fortunate result of this connection was that Riverside Church's famous minister, Harry Emerson Fosdick, became a strong advocate of the early fellowship. Fosdick, whose name is for many synonymous with modernism in American religion, deserves special credit because he was an enthusiastic supporter in the very beginning, even before the Big Book was completed. There's little doubt that his unconditional praise for AA helped open up churches across the country as AA meeting places and also gave the society needed acceptability among many pastors.

Soon afterwards, AA also received the encouragement and help of Father Edward Dowling, a Jesuit from St. Louis, Missouri, and Norman Vincent Peale, whose star was steadily rising as a popular lecturer and pastor of New York's Marble Collegiate Church. Neither Father Dowling nor Dr. Peale would be ranked with Dr. Fosdick as modernists by the people who fret about such definitions. But in the broad historical spectrum of Christian sectarian movements, we would have to regard both more as modernists than traditional fundamentalists. And though some of AA's ideas had come down from evangelicals like Dwight L. Moody and Frank Buchman, the new Twelve Step form was worded so that even the most modern-thinking clergyman could accept it.

AA, though freely using ideas distilled from religious traditions, was never touched by the fundamentalist/modernist controversy in American religion. This ongoing battle still hovers over many denominations today. Closely akin to the liberal/conservative split in politics, it is often so divisive that it paralyzes people in their efforts to work for common improvement in a spirit of harmony. It seems to be a natural division that almost always occurs in organizations and social movements, but it can become poisonous and destructive under some circumstances. Bill Wilson, to his credit, always recognized that AA had its radical/conservative factions, and he also explained how each group was necessary for the preservation and growth of the fellowship.[2]

This profound split in American religion had not occurred in the nineteenth century, when Booth, Finney, and Moody were doing their important work. General Booth was a theological conservative who believed that the earth was created in a mere six calendar days. Finney and Moody had similar views about God and creation, but they also were open-minded and, like Booth, had a great love for humankind. All shared a conviction that repentance, conversion, and a new course of action were necessary for a changed life.

Dwight L. Moody, it was noted in Chapter Nine, had deplored splits that kept the church from helping people, including alcoholics. It was perhaps fortunate that this big-hearted man never really had to deal with the religious/political controversies that split many of his followers in the years after his death. Once, when questioned about the old biblical story of Jonah's being swallowed by the fish, Moody sent a simple telegram stating, "I stand by Jonah."[3] This answer delighted the press and put Moody on the side of those who believed in a strict interpretation of the Bible, but it didn't really settle matters for many people who felt a deep need for God and yet were confused by the Christian scriptures of their upbringing.

Harry Emerson Fosdick rejected such literal interpretations of the Bible, but at the same time believed in God and the mission of Jesus as savior of humankind. He was a lifelong admirer of Dwight L. Moody, and had been influenced by spiritual leaders from the Northfield conferences, some of which he had attended himself. Fosdick believed in a God who is both active in human affairs and responsive to prayer. His Christianity also drew on many Quaker beliefs, particularly its pacifism. He felt that many of the beliefs held by the more established Christian denominations were outdated, however, and he expressed these views in his widely publicized sermons.

A lot of people appreciated Fosdick's open-minded and candid views, which made him one of the most admired ministers in America in the 1930s. But these views also brought condemnation from many Protestant fundamentalists. Though he had critics in his own modernist camp, for these fundamentalists, he came to symbolize the entire camp, even those who had no real spiritual beliefs at all.

Fosdick also became involved with social causes that brought him into sharp contention at times. But he took pride in saying, late in life, "Some good causes with which I have been allied have fortunately been all success without contention—

Alcoholics Anonymous, for example. I teamed up with that movement in its early days, and count my acquaintance with Bill W. . .a very rewarding association." He pointed out that parish pastors had had "the devastating results of alcoholism dumped in our laps day after day—individuals and families ruined by drink, men and women enslaved by a habit they are powerless to break, children humiliated, shamed and irretrievably harmed by drunken parents."[4] Fosdick was so frustrated by the cases of alcoholism he saw that he actually felt gratitude when he learned about AA. Upon publication of *Alcoholics Anonymous* in 1939, Fosdick wrote three praiseful book reviews for religious publications, and he gave the fellowship unstinting support for the rest of his life.

At the same time, Fosdick's Riverside Church, which had been funded by John D. Rockefeller, Jr., and completed in late 1930, served as the conduit for Rockefeller money given to support the AA fellowship. This connection with one of America's most famous ministers and one of New York's most prestigious churches also opened the door to publicity and other opportunities. Fosdick spoke at a large AA gathering in 1941, while Bill Wilson and other AA members were invited to speak at Riverside Church.

AA also appealed to Fosdick because he was interested in any practical application of one's religious beliefs. He was impressed by the spiritual "common ground" AA had been able to establish. "The meetings of Alcoholics Anonymous are the only place, so far as I know, where Roman Catholics, Jews, all kinds of Protestants and even agnostics get together harmoniously on a religious basis," he wrote in 1956. "They do not talk theology. Many of them would say that they know nothing about it. What they do know is that in their utter helplessness they were introduced to a Power, greater than themselves, in contact with whom they found a strong resource which made possible a victory that had seemed incredible. I have listened to many learned arguments about God, but for honest-to-goodness experiential evidence of God, his power personally appropriated and his reality indubitably assured, give me a good meeting of AA!"[5]

Now that more than fifty years has passed since Fosdick gave AA such an enthusiastic early endorsement, it's difficult to understand what this must have meant for Bill Wilson and his still-struggling band of AA pioneers. Getting Fosdick's support was the sort of blessing Bill Wilson would have called a "ten strike." Fosdick, without any urging or second thoughts, had willingly placed his prestige and his great influence behind a tiny movement that could have gone off the tracks and embarrassed him. But like Albert Scott, a lay leader at Riverside Church, Fosdick felt the sincerity and honesty of these recovered alcoholics, and he wanted to see the movement grow. And while Fosdick did not plant any roots for AA's spiritual program, he certainly helped prune and shape its tender branches as it began to grow.

❧   ❧   ❧

Father Edward Dowling, a Jesuit priest from St. Louis, was another clergyman with modern leanings who endorsed, supported, and encouraged the early AA movement. Though Dowling was a traditional Roman Catholic, he had a great capacity for reaching out to other groups at a time when many priests were still narrow and defensive about their beliefs. Impressed by AA's early success—it then had less than a thousand members—Dowling went to New York in 1940 and made a special effort to track down Bill Wilson. They became friends for life, with Dowling often serving as Bill's confidante on matters of great personal concern.[6]

Dowling, who died in 1960, also became Wilson's ally in winning approval of AA by the Roman Catholic hierarchy in the United States. This was no small achievement in the 1940s, when a single negative statement by a Catholic bishop could have placed the fellowship under a dark cloud. Mary Louise Adams, a historian at Maryville College and also the archivist for Dowling's papers, said that without Father Dowling's enthusiastic support, AA might never have achieved acceptance among Catholics so early in its existence.

"At the time many Catholics thought of AA as kind of like the Masons, you know, not for Catholics," Ms. Adams told a *St. Louis Review* writer in 1985. "Father Dowling investigated it thoroughly and thought it was the best thing he'd ever seen to help people with a drinking problem." She went on to say that he had liked AA's grass-roots, democratic nature, its amateurishness—in the positive sense of being non-authoritarian—the way it stressed the union of God and man, and the importance of alcoholics helping themselves. She added, "It wasn't slick or fancy, it just had sincere motives to help people. That's what Father Dowling liked about it."[7]

According to Bill Wilson's account, Father Dowling first came to see him on a rainy night when Bill and Lois were living in the old 24th Street Club in New York—then their only home. The caretaker thought the priest was "a bum from St. Louis" needing help, and it was only when Dowling sat down and turned back his collar that Wilson realized he was a clergyman.

This launched a conversation that lasted for twenty years, Bill Wilson's biography states. They reached an immediate spiritual understanding in their first discussion that night, and Wilson even unburdened himself of problems and fears that were troubling him, speaking of his anger and frustration as well as his aspirations for the tiny AA fellowship.

Dowling, in responding to these concerns, quoted Matthew: "Blessed are they who do hunger and thirst," and pointed out that God's chosen were always distinguished by their yearnings, their restlessness, and their thirst. Nor would there ever be any real satisfaction because there was a "divine dissatisfaction" that would keep Wilson going, "for only by so reaching would he attain what—hidden from him—were God's goals. This acceptance that his dissatisfaction, that his very 'thirst' could be divine was one of Dowling's great gifts to Bill Wilson and through him to Alcoholics Anonymous," Wilson's biography concludes.[8]

Acceptance has indeed become an important spiritual practice in AA, and Dowling, who suffered from crippling arthritis, had known ongoing pain in his own life. While others might have argued that such conditions should be overcome, the gentle Dowling had been forced to live with his infirmities. The AA emphasis on *humility* also may have passed into the fellowship in part through Dowling. He reminded AA members, in a statement that was later used on the Big Book's outer jacket, that "God resists the proud, and assists the humble" and that "humiliations" can be the shortest cut to "humility."

Dowling was also an associate editor of *The Queen's Work*, a magazine published by St. Louis-based Jesuits. This gave him splendid opportunities to publicize AA. Though a non-alcoholic, he carried the AA message to alcoholics, virtually serving as their sponsor, at least to the extent of letting them know about the program. *Pass It On* even credits him with founding AA in St. Louis. He also supported "Recovery" (a Chicago-based group movement founded by Dr. Abraham Low assisting people with emotional problems) and other movements which he considered helpful to troubled human beings.

It's likely, too, that Dowling passed along to Wilson the famous prayer of Saint Francis that was included in the *Twelve Steps and Twelve Traditions,* published in 1953. One of Father Dowling's other contributions was to note that the Twelve Steps actually have deep Christian roots going back to Ignatius Loyola, the fifteenth-century mystic who founded the Jesuits, an order historically known for its intellectualism and high standards.

Loyola, a Basque Spanish nobleman, was a soldier who renounced his profession after a profound spiritual experience. He had other remarkable experiences after periods of intense prayer and fasting, and finally developed a set of Spiritual Exercises aimed at helping his own followers live in closer conformity with God's will. The exercises also followed a weekly schedule or plan and still serve today as important Jesuit guidelines.

Father Dowling, noting that the Twelve Steps are the "real spiritual powerhouse of AA," recalled the astonishment of one Jesuit whom he respected as being wise in the ways of the spirit. Dowling said his colleague was "astounded at the great similarity between those steps and the Foundation and First Week of 'The Spiritual Exercises of St. Ignatius,' which contains the basic and ridding-oneself-of-sin part of Jesuit spirituality."[9]

Dowling's deep interest in AA and other inspirational helping movements was always supplementary to his regular work as a Catholic priest. He always supported and upheld the importance of the formal church organization. As he told AA members at the 1955 AA International Conference in St. Louis, he represented "churchianity." He said that everybody likes Christianity, but people don't always like churchianity, which was a bit like saying that everybody likes water but nobody likes the plumbing that brings it![10]

❧   ❧   ❧

Norman Vincent Peale was a third modern minister to offer AA early, active support. Peale's name became synonymous with *The Power of Positive Thinking* following the 1952 publication of this blockbuster book. This had been preceded, however, by a twenty-year period of active work at New York's Marble Collegiate Church, which served a congregation that included many intelligent young professional and business people. Though Peale always insisted that he was a Christian minister in the old-fashioned, orthodox tradition, he was considered "modernist" by most fundamentalists.

Peale learned about AA in the early 1940s, liked what he saw, and soon became such an enthusiastic supporter that he was invited to address a large AA anniversary banquet a few years later. He was so confident that AA was on the right track that he even stated the belief that future generations would regard Bill Wilson as one of the greatest men of the twentieth century. Later on, Peale devoted much of the closing chapter of *The Power of Positive Thinking* to AA, an endorsement that must have been helpful to the fellowship in view of the book's extraordinary popularity.

Though many AA's may feel that positive thinking and the Twelve Steps are along parallel lines, one member did report, somewhat tongue-in-cheek, that it may have also prolonged his drinking by a few years! Bob P., an advertising executive and writer who later served as general manager of AA World Services, said that he and his wife attended Dr. Peale's church regularly and managed to start each week with helpful affirmations and positive mental attitudes. This produced some nice stretches of hopeful improvement but did not, unfortunately, enable him to sidestep the sneakiness of the first drink or the three-martini lunch.

Finding sobriety in AA a few years later, Bob made the positive thinking period an addition to his personal story, which delighted AA audiences. When he met Peale at a luncheon recently, they both enjoyed Bob's retelling of the experience. Peale also told Bob he had known Bill and Lois well and was a great admirer of the AA program.

Peale, like Dale Carnegie before him, came under attack for offering self-help ideas aimed at improving one's business success. His positive thinking was even dismissed as a form of "cheap grace," using God simply to get what one wants in the world. It was termed an example of trivializing the Gospel, and in the mid-1950s Peale was viciously attacked in print by a number of critics. But he survived all of this to carry on what has been a remarkable speaking and writing career.

Even before Peale became friendly with the pioneering New York AA's, however, he had established many ties to ideas and trends in which the AA program also was rooted. In one book, he told about his experiences in the late 1920s that influenced his thinking. As a young Methodist minister, he was pastor of a Syracuse, New York, church whose congregation included university professors and other well-educated people. He tried to prepare scholarly sermons, which were not being well received, and he felt that his ministry was losing its vitality.

Then he began reading "certain spiritual literature which I had become aware was increasingly pouring into the homes of people in the churches and reaching them, too, with its message.... This material came from the Unity Movement, from Science of Mind, from various metaphysical teachers, from Christian Science, the Oxford Group and Moral Re-Armament. Glenn Clark, Starr Daily and Sam Shoemaker were eagerly read authors," Peale wrote. "These writers taught that Jesus Christ established a scientific, completely workable way of thought and life that brought about change and victory."[11]

Peale found himself making a wonderful new beginning when he wove these ideas into his sermons and church work. He believed he was reaching the deeply felt personal needs of his congregation rather than merely engaging in intellectual exercises. His growing popularity then brought a call to the Marble Church in 1931, where he continued to present the same message. This included much of the "mind-cure" that William James had found so helpful, and many of the Oxford Group teachings that Frank Buchman had developed. Peale also launched a psychiatric clinic at the Marble Church that was much like the Emmanuel Movement in Boston. In cooperation with a psychiatrist named Smiley Blanton, he sought to blend the insights of modern psychotherapy with the principles of religion.

Peale, unlike his good friend Sam Shoemaker, was not acquainted with Bill Wilson while the AA message was developing in the late 1930s. He was a firm ally soon afterwards, however, and his support gave the small fellowship added encouragement at a time when it was most needed. Peale's own spiritual program shared common roots with AA, and he did help prune some of its branches in its early years. Like that given by Harry Emerson Fosdick and Father Edward Dowling, it was the kind of support from active, prominent clergymen that AA needed.

In the nearly half-century that has passed since these ministers gave a helpful boost to the early AA, American religion has undergone profound changes. Harry Emerson Fosdick had believed that his modernist views of Christianity would prevail, but by 1957 Billy Graham replaced him as the country's most popular minister. Graham is not a fundamentalist, but he offers what is essentially the old-time preaching that Fosdick found deficient in so many ways.

Father Dowling's church has gone through monumental upheavals since his death in 1960 and, if anything, is now closer to the ideals he had in mind. Dowling, a loyal Catholic all his life, also wanted the church to be more relevant to human suffering and problems. In some ways, he was a Catholic rebel before his time.

Norman Vincent Peale and Harry Emerson Fosdick were good friends, although they had different opinions about religion. (Fosdick thought Peale's message was excellent, but also believed Peale "had only one string to his bow.") Both believed in the power of God as exemplified in William James's writings, and Fosdick did not join his fellow modernists in attacking Peale in the 1950s.

What all of them believed—Fosdick, Dowling, Peale, and their modern colleagues who endorsed AA—was that God can and does work in human affairs. However they differed on specific doctrines, they were modern advocates of "the first-century Christianity" that Albert Scott had in mind when he commented on the early AA message. They thought of spiritual power and a loving human community as vital and necessary for troubled people. They thought AA was meeting these needs in a wonderful way, and they wanted to see it grow. They were AA's good friends and supporters at a time when their help was most needed.

CHAPTER ELEVEN

AA's Spiritual Program Today

AA and its Twelve Steps are more than fifty-five years old and another century is almost upon us. How well is this movement maintaining its spiritual vitality?

Do AA members still have the strong beliefs in God that moved and guided the society's pioneers? Are the Twelve Steps still the guiding force in AA? Do most members really believe in a Higher Power? Or has it, for many, become part of a ritual merely to pay lip service to the Steps while actually making no real change in thinking or behavior?

Both of AA's co-founders were deeply concerned about the society's long-term survival and effectiveness in helping alcoholics who still suffer. Dr. Bob Smith, in his last appearance before a large AA gathering, advised that the Twelve Steps could be condensed to "love and service" and to hold to these. Bill Wilson always emphasized the importance of AA unity and in sticking to the single purpose of helping alcoholics. His lengthy writing on this subject still guides AA. Bill's words carry as much authority in AA as they did during his lifetime. Members have complete confidence that this man who charted the way with the Twelve Steps knew what was best for the fellowship's future.

But AA could lose much of its spiritual force, even while increasing its numbers, if AA members begin to view it simply as a social service organization rather than a special way of life. AA can survive criticism and even direct attacks, but it would lose its power if its members became lukewarm and indifferent where spiritual matters are concerned.

One way to gauge how members feel is to look at what they say about their spiritual program. Dan J., a thirteen-year member from Bolivia, described AA as being "like a beautiful river." He wrote in 1989, "While AA is like a river, we are a part of that river. We stretch out from the here and now, back to Akron, and also into the future." He added that "the Higher Power expresses himself in our group conscience. When I attend a meeting. . .I meet that Power and learn more about him, about the group, and about myself. I drink from the river and become more fully me."[1]

Kit K., a member from Alaska, also implied a river-like movement in the way AA worked in her life: "I do not understand the flow of people whose paths cross mine in recovery. But I do not need to understand that grand design. If I have faith that my Higher Power is providing for my needs, then I can be confident that those teachers, unlikely as they may appear, are present to contribute to my spiritual growth."[2]

A significant number of AA members still assert that they have trouble believing in a Higher Power, but find help in AA's practice of encouraging members to form a concept of God that will work for them. "I came to AA in such pain that I was willing to do anything to achieve sobriety," a Lufkin, Texas, member wrote. "I was told that the group could be my higher power and I believed it. I then made a decision to turn my will and my life over to the care of whatever there is out there in the universe, if there is anything, that would accept me. Each day when I ask God for another day of sobriety, I understand that I use the concept of God as a metaphor to express my deepest and most vital aspirations."[3]

This cross-section of personal comments shows that AA members' views of their spiritual program are very much like the ideas that enabled early membership to seek a relationship with a Higher Power and build on it. From the very beginning of AA, a large core of its members have taken this view.

It was such a suggestion that helped Bill Wilson put aside his deeply held prejudices against religion, leading to the spiritual experience that changed his life. Many religious leaders would frown on such an application of religious principles, seeing it as a "watering down" of the faith. In AA, however, it survives and helps to maintain a spiritual bond not only among current members, but also with members of the past and into the future.

Despite this broad view of spirituality, AA has not completely escaped criticism. For example, there have been reports that AA members' use of the Lord's Prayer in closing many meetings across the country has been offensive to Jewish and other non-Christian members. Their problem is the Christian origin of the prayer. This objection might rankle some longtime AA members, but it is not an insurmountable problem. As these objections have arisen, the likely AA response would be to discontinue use of the Lord's Prayer and to adopt another prayer or method for closing the meetings. The purpose of AA is to help alcoholics, not simply to promote use of a certain prayer.

AA has also been called a cult, despite Bill Wilson's painstaking efforts to keep it from becoming one. In February 1963, well after AA had become a well-known national institution with a large membership, *Harper's* magazine published a story prominently headlined on its cover: "Alcoholics Anonymous: Cult or Cure?" The author was Arthur H. Cain, a practicing psychologist whose credentials included a Ph.D. from Columbia University and studies at the Yale (now Rutgers) School of Alcohol Studies. The point of his *Harper's* article was that AA, a useful idea, had been turned into a religious movement and had become a hindrance to research, to psychiatry, and to many alcoholics who needed a different kind of help.

But what must have been most disturbing to Bill Wilson was Cain's charge that AA was "becoming one of America's most fanatical religious cults." Cain accused AA members of "intolerance." Apparently disapproving of the large number of AA members who worked in city, state, and private alcoholism agencies, he felt that their views—that is, the AA viewpoint—influenced and also retarded additional research and work in the alcoholism field. He conceded that AA had been and still was helpful to many alcoholics, but he said that AA "dogmatism has prevented many people from seeking a more moderate solution: sobriety in AA without slavery to it."

Many AA members responded to *Harper's* with indignant letters. But acting on AA's behalf, Bill Wilson, instead of making a direct reply to the magazine, prepared a statement titled "Our Critics Can Be Our Benefactors," which was delivered to AA delegates meeting in 1963 and also published in the April 1963 issue of *The AA Grapevine*, the society's publication. Referring to recent criticism that had raised questions about AA's relationships to medicine, religion, and the world at large, Bill reminded members that "we must never become so vain as to suppose that we have been the inventors and authors of a new religion. We will humbly reflect that each of AA's principles, *every one of them*, has been borrowed from ancient sources." He went on to note that it was false pride to believe that AA is a cure-all, even for alcoholism, and he reminded members of their debt to the medical field. He also noted that true criticism could be beneficial, while unjustified attacks should not be opposed. "Unreasonable people are stimulated all the more by opposition," he said.

It had indeed been unreasonable to call AA a cult, but as it turned out, Wilson's nonresponse was the best answer. Two or three critical articles followed, and then the attacks subsided. And while some critics may still view AA as a cult, it is not so regarded by the general public.

But its spiritual program, though greatly diluted from the assertive evangelism of the Oxford Group, has still been too strong for some critics. It must have surprised people at AA World Services when B. F. Skinner, the celebrated behaviorist, now deceased, sent in a humanistic alternative to AA's Twelve Steps. Dr. Skinner's step program, which eliminated any reference to God or a Power Greater than Ourselves, was published in the July/August 1987 issue of *The Humanist.* "Several people have told me that they turned to Alcoholics Anonymous for help but have been offended by its heavily religious character," Dr. Skinner explained. He said he sent his version of the steps to AA, suggesting that they offer it as an alternative for nonreligious members. "I was not suggesting that they abandon their own twelve steps. I was told, however, that it would be impossible to change their practices without a majority vote of all Alcoholics Anonymous and was assured that many atheists and agnostics have found the original twelve steps helpful." Skinner offered his steps for humanist counselors who might like to use them.

It's doubtful that AA's reply suited Dr. Skinner, but it is true that atheists and agnostics survive in AA and find some benefit in the steps. J.L., of El Granada, California, says that he is an atheist with long-term sobriety in the AA program. He admits that he was uncomfortable with the references to God and a Higher Power, but his need for help and his open-mindedness won out, and he also discovered that "all that God talk had not injured me." He eventually realized that the Steps—even those that include God—offered a rational way to think and live. "I find I actually do very little that is different from the actions of those who believe in God," he says. "I just think about the actions in a different way."[4]

J.L.'s ability to work within the framework of AA's Twelve Steps isn't shared by everybody, however, and two alternative societies recently have appeared that eliminate references to a Higher Power. According to a May 27, 1990, story in the *Detroit Free Press,* one of these groups is Secular Organizations for Sobriety, or SOS. The other is Rational Recovery. Both appear to share the humanist approach advocated by Dr. Skinner.

Secular Organizations for Sobriety, according to the report, was founded by Jim Christopher, who authored two books: *How to Stay Sober: Recovery Without Religion* and *Unhooked: Staying Sober and Drug-Free.* Christopher is said to call the group a friendly alternative to AA, and has members who go to both groups' meetings.

Rational Recovery, founded by a Wayne State University graduate named Jack Trimpey, is said to represent a "true ideological split with AA." Trimpey was quoted by *Detroit Free Press* writer Judy Rose as saying that his group was "trying to protect people from further exposure to [AA's] doctrine of submissiveness and powerlessness, which is very damaging to mental health."

While both SOS and Rational Recovery object to AA's reliance on God and a Higher Power, the Twelve Steps have come under fire for a third reason. Gail Unterberger, who teaches pastoral care and counseling at Wesley Theological Seminary in Washington, D.C., has written that the Steps "insinuate a hierarchical, domination-submission model of the individual's relationship to God. God is always referred to as male, and God's activities are described in stereotypically masculine terms." Further objections to the Steps included the admission of powerlessness, guilt, and wrongdoing, and the need for a humble plea for power as well as prayer and meditation. "The addict is a lone ranger on a personal spiritual journey," Ms. Unterberger noted, "albeit a journey paralleling that of others." She then supplied a version of the Steps that eliminated the masculine references which she and other feminists found objectionable.[5]

But if some people found AA's program too Christian or religious, others require an approach that is more explicitly attuned to evangelical Christian values. Alcoholics for Christ and Alcoholics Victorious are two new fellowships that utilize the basic understandings of AA but relate it more closely to biblical references and evangelical Christian teachings. By way of example, Alcoholics for Christ revises several of the AA steps to include Jesus Christ and also eliminates the more general "God as we understood Him." Alcoholics for Christ retains a friendly approach to AA, however, and urges its members to continue attending AA meetings and to attend their own churches.[6]

No comment about any of these new approaches to recovery is likely to come from AA World Services, because the fellowship does not issue opinions on such issues. But since Bill Wilson always warned that AA did not have the only answer to alcoholism and should cooperate with other groups, his response no doubt would be to wish all such ventures well. As one AA member put it when questioned about a new form of AA meetings, "I'm for anything that helps alcoholics recover!" And with alcoholism still the leading form of addiction in most parts of the civilized world, it's clear that there may be need for additional approaches to recovery.

It is remarkable, however, that the new groups tend to focus on certain of the fundamental ideas that contributed to AA's beginnings, or the ideas that fed into the Oxford Group. Rational Recovery, for example, gives much force to the use of human reason in dealing with problems. Richard Peabody, in *The Common Sense of Drinking,* certainly offered an approach that appealed to the individual's reasoning powers. He was also influenced by the insights of Sigmund Freud, Alfred Adler, and Carl Jung, all of whom relied on reason in varying ways. Even William James applied reason in *The Varieties of Religious Experience.*

Alcoholics for Christ, though advocating a spiritual approach that would be too blatantly Christian and evangelical for many AA members, is surprisingly close in tone to Jerry McAuley, Dwight L. Moody, and other evangelists who formed some of AA's early roots. There is a direct link between Moody and the current fundamentalists and evangelicals who helped popularize the born-again movement of the 1970s. With AA, they share the belief that troubled human beings may at times be completely unable to aid themselves, with or without the help of other human beings. An alcoholic who attributes his recovery to Jesus Christ is simply being more specific than an AA member who defines God "as we understood Him."

And what about referring to God or the Higher Power as "Him"? Despite Ms. Unterberger's objections, this practice is likely to continue for a time in AA, if only because members are loath to change anything that appears to be functioning with reasonable success. Such masculine terms abound in the AA Big Book and other early AA literature, not only with reference to God but also in describing alcoholics. This is due in part to the fact that such references were in common use in 1939, when the Big Book was written; the masculine pronouns were then considered to include both genders. It was also true, though, that the first hundred or so alcoholics involved in preparing the Big Book for publication, except for one, were men, and the plight of the woman alcoholic was not addressed with equal success by the *fellow*ship for some years to come. Now that these practices are no longer acceptable, it's likely that AA will eventually have gender-neutral terms in most of its literature and, someday, perhaps even in the Twelve Steps.

This is easily predictable because AA World Services, reflecting the conciliatory spirit of the society's co-founders, is continuously moving to accommodate any reasonable need or point of view in the fellowship. Guided by the principle of reaching the alcoholic who still suffers, AA moves out to welcome alcoholics who belong to populations who have been scorned or rejected by the larger society. In line with its traditions, AA has been consistent in neither opposing nor supporting political and social causes. But it has taken reasonable steps to carry the AA message to the people involved in such causes.

Almost from the earliest years, for example, AA members and groups have aided the establishment of AA in prisons. It has also reached out to African-American members, even in the days when racial segregation and prejudice made it difficult to invite minority members to meetings. AA sought to make its program more inclusive of and acceptable to women, although it is still often accused of being male-dominated. Although not officially sanctioned by the General Service Board, many women-only and men-only groups have sprung up around the country to address these members' special needs. A growing awareness of alcoholic problems among Native Americans also evoked a special AA response, as evidenced by a pamphlet, *AA for the Native North American*, issued by AA World Services.

Furthermore, AA World Services released a pamphlet for gay/lesbian alcoholics, thus taking a stand, of sorts, on one of society's most sensitive issues. In AA as elsewhere, homosexuals were often condemned in the 1940s and 1950s, but such prejudice began to soften in the 1960s and 1970s with the appearance of special groups designed for gay men and lesbian women. Frank Buchman and the Oxford Group, like many evangelicals, had looked upon homosexuality as something that could and should be adjusted by spiritual means. AA takes no such stands and has simply moved to assure gays and lesbians that AA's chief concern is only in helping them deal with their drinking problems.

In moving with changing times, however, it's not likely that AA will consider modifying its Twelve Steps or any of its spiritual ideas in the program of action. While some critics such as the late B. F. Skinner may view this spiritual content as excess baggage that could be discarded, AA members still believe these principles are the foundation of AA's success in helping alcoholics.

And while some outside professionals may view AA's spiritual program simply as a means of changing oneself psychologically, AA members still believe that some kind of Divine Intervention is at work in the program. An honest desire to seek help, an open-mindedness about spirituality, and only a slight willingness to give it a chance in one's life are the only essentials for a beginning. For many, this has opened the door to a deep and lasting spiritual life.

A member in Belgium, for example, found sobriety without the degree of happiness he was truly seeking. He followed his sponsor's advice to "try" to come to a belief and faith in a Higher Power.

"I began to be aware of the presence of the Higher Power in every AA meeting," he later reported. "I believe the Higher Power speaks through the mouths of the friends who sit at my side. The Higher Power makes me happy with the warm handshake of my AA friends. The Higher Power helps me remain sober."[7]

A Higher Power is still believed to be directing people to AA in marvelous ways, even as in AA's pioneering times. Fred B., a member from Germany, described the terrors of a ten-day bender in which he almost killed himself and others in a car accident. After the bender, he fell on his knees praying aloud for God's help. The next morning, he read in the local paper that AA had just been established in his hometown. He attended his first German AA meeting in September 1967 and has not had a drink since. "I am a grateful recovering alcoholic today," he wrote recently. "I am in harmony with others and the universe, because I have accepted and forgiven myself, knowing that lifelong remorse and self-condemnation would only endanger my hard-earned sobriety."[8]

AA members also find their Higher Power to be a source of strength when facing impossible situations in sobriety. One young woman discovered that she had tested positive for the AIDS virus, having been infected by her ex-boyfriend. Writing about this without resentment or self-pity, she explained how she had been able to come to terms with it, using the principles of the program. "Life is an experience meant to be lived," she wrote, "taking risks and knowing that the results are being cared for through our Higher Power."[9]

If AA's co-founders could return to read such comments today, there's little doubt that they'd feel confident and secure about the fellowship's spiritual program. The Twelve Steps are still in good hands, even in a fellowship that is now world-wide and has seen vast change since the early words about spirituality were written in the AA Big Book in 1937 to 1939. Whatever arguments might be mounted against AA and its spirit-based program, the central fact of AA life is that it works and continues to work for the thousands who follow it.

There may also be a very simple explanation for the continuing importance of the spiritual program to AA's membership. Carl Jung, in responding to Bill Wilson's letter of gratitude, recalled how he had felt that Rowland H.'s drinking was, in reality, a need for God operating at a very low level. In drinking, this deeply felt, eternal need is being met in false and destructive ways, and the alcoholic is the victim of an evil principle "that is very aptly called the Devil."

Following Jung's simple Latin formula, *spiritus contra spiritum,* AA members meet this deeply felt spiritual need in peaceful and constructive ways, following principles that have their Source in a Higher Power that is called, very aptly, God as we understood Him. "The Spirit of God overcomes the power of alcohol."

Epilogue—
Is AA a World-Changing
Fellowship?

AA's continuing success in helping alcoholics to sobriety led some of the society's admirers to believe the Twelve Steps could help save the troubled world.

But Bill Wilson always warned AA members not to entertain such notions. A shoemaker should stick to his last, he argued, and AA's mission was only to help alcoholics, not to reform the world. He was so firm in this principle that he even opposed accepting drug-addicted persons into AA unless they also showed signs of alcoholism. He stated his belief with complete clarity in remarks at the second international convention of AA, in St. Louis, in 1955:

> There are those who predict that Alcoholics Anonymous may well become a new spearhead for a spiritual awakening throughout the world. When our friends say these things they are both generous and sincere. But we of AA must reflect that such a tribute and such a prophecy could well prove to be a heady drink for most of us—that is, if we really came to believe this to be the real purpose of AA, and if we commenced to behave accordingly. Our society, therefore, will prudently cleave to its single purpose: the carrying of the message to the alcoholic who still suffers. Let us resist the proud assumption that since God has enabled us to do well in one area we are destined to be a channel of saving grace for everybody.[1]

Despite this disclaimer, Bill Wilson did feel that AA's program was applicable to world problems. His widow, Lois, revealed that both of them had privately held hope that the

AA program would reach beyond alcoholism. "I believed, as Bill did, that if he could find a way to give others what he had, he would begin something that would have the power to change the world," Lois said in 1985, addressing AA's fiftieth anniversary convention in Montreal. "Bill and I always believed that, as more and more people embrace our way of life and reach out in love to others, the principles on which our fellowship is based will one day save our troubled world."[2]

One way AA is doing that is to share its program freely with other societies based on mutual self-help. This is fully in keeping with Bill Wilson's general spirit of cooperating with the world outside of AA. In the same St. Louis talk where he insisted AA should cleave to its single purpose of helping alcoholics, Bill Wilson left the door open for such cooperation. He endorsed the idea of sharing AA's experience and spirit "for whatever it may be worth, to the world around us."

Following AA's example, people suffering from various problems have created what amounts to an explosion of "Anonymous" activity. This has become so prevalent that "Anonymous" itself has come to mean a helping society. There is a Gamblers Anonymous, an Overeaters Anonymous, a Cocaine Anonymous, and a Narcotics Anonymous. Additionally, there is a Parents Anonymous (for parents abusive to their children), a Sex Addicts Anonymous, an Emotions Anonymous, and a Workaholics Anonymous. All of these programs—and this is only a partial listing—apply the basic Twelve Steps and Twelve Traditions, with AA's permission.

One could say that the troubled world is already partly saved when alcoholics and other sick people recover from their compulsions and addictions. But people who want to remake the world would be impatient with the Twelve Step approach of working with only one person at a time. It can also be exasperating that "Anonymous" societies extend their help only to those who appear to want it. If the Twelve Step principles can solve world problems, what can be done to persuade more people to accept them?

Frank Buchman certainly had such accelerated world-changing in mind with the Oxford Group and its successor fellowship, Moral Re-Armament. Indeed, *Remaking the World* was the title of a book of his speeches published in 1961, the year of his death. In a speech titled "America, Awake!" he outlined this purpose:

> The Oxford Group is a Christian revolution for remaking the world. The root problems in the world today are dishonesty, selfishness and fear—in men and, consequently, in nations. These evils multiplied result in divorce, crime, unemployment, recurrent depression and war. How can we hope for peace within a nation, or between nations, when we have conflict in countless homes? Spiritual recovery must precede economic recovery. Political or social solutions that do not deal with these root problems are inadequate. Manmade laws are no substitute for individual character. Our instant need is a moral and spiritual awakening. Human wisdom alone has failed to bring this about. It is only possible when God has control of individuals.[3]

Similar thoughts have been expressed from time to time by other spiritual leaders, and it's common to hear people voice the belief that following the Golden Rule and the simple precepts of the Sermon on the Mount would change the world for the better. Since AA, through the Oxford Group, embraced these ancient principles which, in Bill Wilson's words, are "the common property of mankind," why aren't more people and nations using this property for promoting peace and general improvement?

The fundamental problem, as Lois Wilson revealed in her Montreal remarks, is in *finding a way to give others what AA has.* This is no small assignment, and it is still beyond the means available to AA or any of the mutual self-help groups that grew out of it. AA is not alone in facing this problem. There are many worthy religious and personal improvement societies whose

New Wine

beliefs might benefit large numbers of troubled people. But as AA has discovered in its single mission of helping alcoholics, there must be a willingness to change before any help can be given and received.

There is also another problem in deliberate efforts to change others: Even when we make the slightest hint that the other person or group needs to accept our ideas for self-improvement, a barrier goes up. Nobody likes to be demeaned by being preached at in a finger-pointing manner. And almost no one likes the self-righteous, arrogant attitude that often goes hand in hand with programs to reform others.

Bill Wilson and the early AA members discovered this almost by chance in their phrasing of the Twelve Steps. The earlier versions told the alcoholic what he needed to do in order to recover. The kinder, gentler way that finally appeared merely said, in effect, "Here is what *we* did to recover, and we offer it to you only as a suggestion."

A second problem is that recovering alcoholics in AA offer a good example of people who overcame severe drinking problems, but may continue to face other problems that they cannot solve in their own lives. The AA program was not designed to nor does it appear to keep many people from divorcing, for example; and individual members often continue to suffer from family estrangements, job difficulties, and personal depression. Bill Wilson was himself personally devastated by a profound depression that at times nearly destroyed him over a long period. Facing so many problems of their own, AA members would hardly be fitted for any role as true world-changers. And yet, how many of these foibles and struggles are simply part of the human condition, whether one is alcoholic or not?

On a larger scale, AA offers no explicit pattern for the governance and security of nations in a warring world. Frank Buchman and his Oxford Group/MRA associates were strongly convinced that they could remake the world—and bring about true peace—by converting its influential, powerful leaders. Others believe, however, that the leaders at any given time

170

simply represent strong currents of feelings held by their people, and this is what must change to bring about true peace.

Whatever one chooses to believe about solutions for world problems, however, it's almost certain that neither AA nor the world is likely to benefit from any change in the society's mission. As Bill Wilson shrewdly and wisely said, "it could well prove to be a heady drink" for most AA members if they really came to believe that such world-changing is the real purpose of AA, and if they commenced to act accordingly. He knew from past experience that people might greatly admire what AA has accomplished, but would likely resent any suggestion that ex-drunks know what is best for others. Recovering alcoholics discover that such missionary efforts don't even work with their own family members and friends, to say nothing of applying them to the larger world.

If AA does have anything to offer in changing or remaking the world, it may be in providing an example of using ancient spiritual ideas to solve seemingly hopeless problems in modern times. The foundation of this message may be the simple Three-Step process outlined in the AA Big Book and read at most AA meetings: "(a) that we were alcoholic and could not manage our own lives, (b) that probably no human power could have relieved our alcoholism, and (c) that God could and would if He were sought."[4] Put in more universal language, this simply comes out as: (1) admission of failure in managing our own affairs, (2) realizing that a solution may be *humanly* impossible, and (3) recognizing and seeking the aid of a Higher Power.

This is essentially what most of the "Anonymous" groups have done in dealing with their own forms of defeat. AA, as the pilot society for such efforts, is in the favored position of receiving credit for their successes while having no responsibility for any failures and problems they may have. It is also remarkable that these various societies have arisen without any promotion or missionary work by AA to extend its influence into other fields. The key element has been "attraction"—doing something good that works well, and thus inspiring others to accept it and use it in their own lives.

So if AA is to engage in world-changing, it will continue to be by attraction and example—not by mounting what could be a clumsy and ill-starred effort to give AA's program universal distribution. Bill Wilson would probably have liked nothing more than to see AA's ancient spiritual principles applied in all human affairs. But he explained in 1955 that AA members could only hope that the society would lead to "better things for those who suffer from alcoholism; that the lessons and examples of our experience may in some measure bring comfort and assurance to the suffering and confused world about us, the world in which it is our privilege to be alive in this exciting and perilous time, this century in which spiritual rebirth may be the only alternative to extinction."[5]

Endnotes

Introduction: What Do AA Members Believe?

1. Wilson's and Smith's surnames were publicly disclosed after their deaths.
2. *Alcoholics Anonymous*, 3rd ed. (New York: Alcoholics Anonymous World Services, Inc., 1976), 25.
3. Ibid., 181.
4. *Alcoholics Anonymous Comes of Age* (New York: Alcoholics Anonymous World Services, Inc., 1957), 197.
5. *Alcoholics Anonymous*, 46.
6. Emmet Fox, *Alter Your Life* (New York: Harper, 1950), 149.
7. Jack H. Mendelson and Nancy K. Mello, *Alcohol—Use and Abuse in America* (Boston: Little Brown, 1985), 338.
8. Alexis Carrel, *Man the Unknown* (New York: Harper, 1935), 44-50.

Chapter One: An Overdue Letter to Dr. Carl Jung

1. Letter to C.G. Jung from Bill W. Copyright © 1963, 1991, by The AA Grapevine, Inc.; reprinted with permission.
2. Ibid.
3. *The Language of the Heart* (New York, AA Grapevine, Inc., 1988), 280-281.
4. Ibid., 282.
5. Carl G. Jung, *Modern Man in Search of a Soul* (New York: Harcourt, Brace, 1933), 277.
6. Letter to C.G. Jung from Bill W., AA Grapevine, Inc.
7. Verified by author in discussion with T. Willard Hunter, 9 Aug. 1990.
8. Cebra G., interviewed by Bill W., 1954 (AA Archives).
9. Rowland H. to Charles S. D. of Denver, 1 Mar. 1937. Letter supplied by Bill Pittman.
10. Bob Scott, interviewed by author, 4 Nov. 1981.
11. Edwin ("Ebby") T., interviewed by Bill W., June 1954 (AA Archives).

12. *Pass It On* (New York: Alcoholics Anonymous World Services, Inc., 1984), 115.

13. Ibid., 120-121.

14. Ibid., 123.

15. Letter to C.G. Jung from Bill W., AA Grapevine, Inc.

16. *Alcoholics Anonymous*, 60.

17. Letter to C.G. Jung from Bill W., AA Grapevine, Inc.

Chapter Two: What Was the Oxford Group?

1. Bill Wilson, in answer to question by author, in 1961.

2. *Pass It On*, 386-387.

3. This can easily be inferred from Alexander's letter to Wilson discussing clearance.

4. *Alcoholics Anonymous Comes of Age*, 39.

5. T. Willard Hunter, conversation with author, 9 Aug. 1990.

6. Garth Lean, *On the Tail of a Comet* (Colorado Springs, Colo.: Helmers & Howard, 1988), 3.

7. Ibid., 27.

8. Ibid., 30.

9. Mark O. Guldseth, *Streams* (Fritz Creek, Alaska.: Fritz Creek Studios, 1982).

10. A. J. Russell, *For Sinners Only* (New York: Harper, 1932), 42-44.

11. T. Willard Hunter, *World Changing Through Life Changing* (Andover, Mass.: Andover Newton Theological School, 1977), 13-14.

12. Ibid., 15.

13. Peter Howard, *Frank Buchman's Secret* (Garden City, N.Y.: Doubleday, 1961).

14. Information in Richmond Walker correspondence at Hazelden Educational Services, Center City, Minn.

15. Jim Newton, conversation with author, March 1990.

16. Shep C., telephone interview by author, 1980.

17. Harold Begbie, *More Twice-Born Men* (New York: Putnam, 1923).

18. Ibid.

19. Henry P. Van Dusen, *The Atlantic Monthly* (August 1934).

20. *Alcoholics Anonymous Comes of Age*, 160.

21. John W. Drakeford, *People to People Therapy* (New York: Harper & Row, 1978), 26.

22. Hunter believes that Buchman said this in connection with the decision of the Akron group to withdraw from the Oxford Group movement.

Chapter Three: Dr. Sam

1. Irving Harris, *The Breeze of the Spirit* (New York: Seabury Press, 1978), 3-5.

2. Helen Smith Shoemaker, *I Stand By the Door* (New York: Harper & Row, 1967), 26.

3. Ibid., 26.

4. *Pass It On*, 130.

5. *Alcoholics Anonymous Comes of Age*, 261-271.

6. William James, *The Varieties of Religious Experience* (New York: Modern Library, 1936), 198-199.

7. Shoemaker, *I Stand By the Door*, 189-190.

8. Russell, *For Sinners Only*, 179-180.

9. *Pass It On*, 116-119.

10. Shoemaker, *I Stand By the Door*, 59-60.

11. Lean, *On the Tail of a Comet*, 304.

12. Sam Shoemaker, letter to Bill Wilson, 27 June 1949 (New York: AA Archives).

13. Shoemaker, *I Stand by the Door*, 219-220.

Chapter Four: Setting the Stage in Akron

1. *Alcoholics Anonymous*, 178.

2. James D. Newton, *Uncommon Friends* (New York: Harcourt Brace Jovanovich, 1987), 152-156.

3. James D. Newton, interview with author, July 1981.

4. Ibid.

5. Ibid.

6. G. E. Hancock, "Testimony Is Given by Firestones," *Akron Beacon Journal*, 21 Jan. 1933.

7. *Pass It On*, 145.

8. Bill D., conversation with author, November 1952.

9. *Silent* may really have been *secret*, the word used in *Dr. Bob and the Good Oldtimers* (New York: Alcoholics Anonymous World Services, Inc., 1980), 58.

10. Dorothy Seiberling Steinberg, interviewed by author, 1981.

11. *Pass It On*, 137.

12. *Dr. Bob and the Good Oldtimers*, 128-136.

Chapter Five: Bill Wilson's Hot Flash

1. Richard Maurice Bucke, *Cosmic Consciousness* (New York: Dutton, 1923).

2. Bill Wilson to author, 2 July 1956.

3. *Alcoholics Anonymous*, 14. The "proposals" referred to in this quotation are essentially the suggestions that later came to be developed as the Twelve Steps.

4. James, *The Varieties of Religious Experience*, 390-391.

5. Bucke, *Cosmic Consciousness*, 72-74.

6. Ibid., 383-384.

7. Clarence W. Hall, *Samuel Logan Brengle, Portrait of a Prophet* (New York: Salvation Army, 1933), 52.

8. Francis Younghusband, *The Heart of Nature* (New York: E.P. Dutton, 1922), 168.

9. Cecil Osborne, *The Art of Understanding Yourself* (Grand Rapids, Mich.: Zondervan House, 1967), 206-207.

10. *Alcoholics Anonymous*, 13-14.

11. Ibid., 14.

12. Norman Vincent Peale, *Inspiring Messages for Daily Living* (Englewood Cliffs, N.J.: Prentice-Hall, 1955), 27.

13. *Alcoholics Anonymous*, 14.

14. Bucke, *Cosmic Consciousness*, 100-101.

15. Bill Wilson to author, 2 July 1956.

16. Ibid.

Chapter Six: Breaking with the Oxford Group

1. *Lois Remembers* (New York: Al-Anon Family Group Headquarters, 1979), 103-104.
2. *Pass It On*, 178.
3. Bob Scott, interviewed by author at Michigan State University, East Lansing, 1981.
4. *Lois Remembers*, 103.
5. Hunter, *World Changing Through Life Changing*, 44. This point was also discussed with Hunter by telephone on 10 April 1990.
6. Ibid., 41.
7. Clarence S., letter to the editor, *Cleveland Press*, 21 Feb. 1941.
8. *Alcoholics Anonymous Comes of Age*, 141.
9. *Dr. Bob and the Good Oldtimers*, 218.
10. *Alcoholics Anonymous Comes of Age*, 75.
11. *Pass It On*, 173.
12. Lean, *On the Tail of a Comet*, 1-2.
13. *Alcoholics Anonymous*, 16.

Chapter Seven: Mutual Self-Help Ideas Were in the Air

1. Alexis de Tocqueville, *Democracy in America* (New York: Mentor Books, New American Library, 1956), 200-202. As we know today, the Washingtonian movement, whose forerunners served as such a striking example for Tocqueville, did not survive, though by some reports it helped at least 150,000 alcoholics find permanent recovery. In its beginnings, it was very similar to AA in focusing on the individual alcoholic's recovery rather than political and social issues. For that, it won Abraham Lincoln's admiration. Bill Wilson also felt that AA profited by avoiding the mistakes that had caused the Washingtonians' collapse.
2. *Alcoholics Anonymous*, 14.
3. James, *The Varieties of Religious Experience*, 108.
4. *Alcoholics Anonymous*, 2nd ed. (New York: Alcoholics Anonymous Publishing, 1955), 341.
5. *Lois Remembers*, 84.
6. *Pass It On*, 230-231.

7. James, *The Varieties of Religious Experience*, 113.

8. Ralph Waldo Trine, *In Tune with the Infinite* (Indianapolis-New York: Bobbs-Merrill, 1947, from 1897 edition).

9. Charles S. Braden, *Spirits in Rebellion* (Dallas: Southern Methodist University Press, 1963), 26.

10. Trine, *In Tune with the Infinite*, 16.

11. Fox, *Alter Your Life*, 149. As an example, Fox spoke of "consciously contacting" God.

12. Richard M. Huber, *The American Idea of Success* (New York: McGraw-Hill, 1971), 181.

13. Leslie D. Weatherhead, *Psychology, Religion and Healing* (New York: Abingdon Press, 1951), 122-128.

14. C. Harry Brooks, *The Practice of Autosuggestion* (New York: Dodd, Mead, 1922), 63.

15. Ibid., 118-119.

16. Huber, *The American Idea of Success*, 181-185.

17. Braden, *Spirits in Rebellion*, 354-355.

18. *Dr. Bob and the Good Oldtimers*, 310-311.

19. Dale Carnegie, *How to Win Friends and Influence People* (New York: Simon & Schuster, 1936), 124-125.

20. Alexis de Tocqueville, *Democracy in America*, 201.

Chapter Eight: Richard Peabody
And the Emmanuel Movement

1. Francis Chambers and Edward A. Strecker, *Alcohol: One Man's Meat* (New York: Macmillan, 1938).

2. Richard R. Peabody, *The Common Sense of Drinking* (Boston: Little, Brown, 1931), 99.

3. Katherine McCarthy, "Early Alcoholism Treatment: The Emmanuel Movement and Richard Peabody," *Journal of Studies on Alcohol* (January 1984): 59.

4. Weatherhead, *Psychology, Religion and Healing*, 221.

5. McCarthy, "Early Alcoholism Treatment," 59.

6. Caresse Crosby, *The Passionate Years* (New York: Ecco Press, 1979), 91-92.

7. Peabody, *The Common Sense of Drinking*, 188-199.

8. McCarthy, "Early Alcoholism Treatment," 61.

9. The original Peabody model of individual therapy died out in the early 1950s; however, one opinion has it that a Peabody therapist, Raymond G. McCarthy, modified individual therapy into a group method and used it for the Yale Plan clinics in Connecticut, which became the model for many rehabilitation clinics around the country.

Chapter Nine: AA's Roots in Old-Time Religion

1. Arthur Bonner, *Jerry McAuley and His Mission* (Neptune, N.J.: Loizeaux Brothers, 1967), 16-17.

2. Ibid., 22-24.

3. Ibid., 11.

4. General William Booth, *In Darkest England and the Way Out* (London: Charles Knight, 1970), 180-187.

5. Harold Begbie, *Twice-Born Men* (New York: Fleming H. Revell, 1909).

6. Guldseth, *Streams*, 118-119. Buchman met Booth-Clibborn at Keswick in 1938, and this may have been confused with the time of his conversion, thirty years earlier. Jessie Penn-Lewis was not a Salvationist, but she shared the Army's evangelical beliefs.

7. Begbie, *Twice-Born Men*, 15-22.

8. Ernest Kurtz, *Not-God: A History of Alcoholics Anonymous* (Center City, Minn.: Hazelden Educational Materials, 1979), 183.

9. Guldseth, *Streams*, 64.

10. Ibid., 66-73.

11. James Findlay, "Dwight L. Moody, American Evangelist," *Encyclopedia of World Biography* (New York: McGraw-Hill, 1973), 7: 498-499.

12. Ibid.

13. Guldseth, *Streams*, 26.

14. Robert E. Speer, *The Principles of Jesus* (New York: Fleming H. Revell, 1902), 33-36.

15. George Stewart, Jr., *Life of Henry B. Wright* (New York: Association Press, 1925), 18.

16. William R. Moody, *The Life of Dwight L. Moody* (New York: Fleming H. Revell, 1900), 497-498.

Chapter Ten: AA's Boosters in the Modern Church

1. *Alcoholics Anonymous Comes of Age*, 148.
2. *The Language of the Heart*, 10-12, 88, 219.
3. Moody, *The Life of Dwight L. Moody*, 496.
4. Harry Emerson Fosdick, *The Living of These Days* (New York: Harper, 1956), 286-287.
5. Ibid., 287-288.
6. *Pass It On*, 241-243.
7. Paul Pennick, Jr., "Alcoholics Anonymous Celebrates 50 Years," *St. Louis Review* (2 Aug. 1985).
8. *Pass It On*, 241-243.
9. Father Edward Dowling, interviewed by Frank A. Riley in the periodical *The Queen's Work*, 1947.
10. *Alcoholics Anonymous Comes of Age*, 258.
11. Norman Vincent Peale, *The Tough-Minded Optimist* (Englewood Cliffs, N.J.: Prentice-Hall, 1961), 32.

Chapter Eleven: AA's Spiritual Program Today

1. Dan J., "Fullness of Life," *AA Grapevine*, April 1989.
2. Kit K., "Unlikely Teachers," *AA Grapevine*, April 1990.
3. J.C., "God as a Metaphor," *AA Grapevine*, April 1988.
4. J.L., "A Program of Action," *AA Grapevine*, March 1989.
5. Gail Unterberger, "Twelve Steps for Women Alcoholics," *The Christian Century*, 106 (6 Dec. 1989): 1150-1152.
6. From information supplied by Alcoholics for Christ, Inc., 1316 North Campbell Road, Royal Oak, MI 48067.
7. Romain B., "Happily Sober," *AA Grapevine*, July 1990.
8. Fred B., "The Best Years of My Life," *AA Grapevine*, July 1990.
9. "Only Love Has Meaning," *AA Grapevine*, June 1989.

Epilogue: Is AA a World-Changing Fellowship?

1. *Alcoholics Anonymous Comes of Age*, 232.
2. Reported by T. Willard Hunter in letter to author, 20 July 1990.
3. Frank N. D. Buchman, *Remaking the World* (London: Blandford Press, 1961), 28.
4. *Alcoholics Anonymous*, 60.
5. *Alcoholics Anonymous Comes of Age*, 231.

THE TWELVE STEPS
OF ALCOHOLICS ANONYMOUS*

1. We admitted we were powerless over alcohol—that our lives had become unmanageable.
2. Came to believe that a Power greater than ourselves could restore us to sanity.
3. Made a decision to turn our will and our lives over to the care of God *as we understood Him*.
4. Made a searching and fearless moral inventory of ourselves.
5. Admitted to God, to ourselves, and to another human being the exact nature of our wrongs.
6. Were entirely ready to have God remove all these defects of character.
7. Humbly asked Him to remove our shortcomings.
8. Made a list of all persons we had harmed, and became willing to make amends to them all.
9. Made direct amends to such people wherever possible, except when to do so would injure them or others.
10. Continued to take personal inventory and when we were wrong promptly admitted it.
11. Sought through prayer and meditation to improve our conscious contact with God *as we understood Him*, praying only for knowledge of His will for us and the power to carry that out.
12. Having had a spiritual awakening as the result of these steps, we tried to carry this message to alcoholics, and to practice these principles in all our affairs.

---

*The Twelve Steps of A.A. are taken from *Alcoholics Anonymous*, 3rd ed., published by A.A. World Services, Inc., New York, N.Y., 59-60. Reprinted with permission of A.A. World Services, Inc.

THE TWELVE TRADITIONS
OF ALCOHOLICS ANONYMOUS*

1. Our common welfare should come first; personal recovery depends upon A.A. unity.
2. For our group purpose there is but one ultimate authority—a loving God as He may express Himself in our group conscience. Our leaders are but trusted servants; they do not govern.
3. The only requirement for A.A. membership is a desire to stop drinking.
4. Each group should be autonomous except in matters affecting other groups or A.A. as a whole.
5. Each group has but one primary purpose—to carry its message to the alcoholic who still suffers.
6. An A.A. group ought never endorse, finance or lend the A.A. name to any related facility or outside enterprise, lest problems of money, property and prestige divert us from our primary purpose.
7. Every A.A. group ought to be fully self-supporting, declining outside contributions.
8. Alcoholics Anonymous should remain forever nonprofessional, but our service centers may employ special workers.
9. A.A., as such, ought never be organized; but we may create service boards or committees directly responsible to those they serve.
10. Alcoholics Anonymous has no opinion on outside issues; hence the A.A. name ought never be drawn into public controversy.
11. Our public relations policy is based on attraction rather than promotion; we need always maintain personal anonymity at the level of press, radio and films.
12. Anonymity is the spiritual foundation of all our Traditions, ever reminding us to place principles before personalities.

---

*The Twelve Traditions of A.A. are taken from *Alcoholics Anonymous*, 3rd ed., published by A.A. World Services, Inc., New York, N.Y., 564. Reprinted with permission of AA. World Services, Inc.

Index

A

AA. *See* Alcoholics Anonymous

AA for the Native North American, 163

AA Grapevine: article about Frank Buchman for, 27, 28; Bill Wilson's response to criticism in, 158; Carl Jung's letter in, 10; memorial to Sam Shoemaker in, 56, 59

AA World Services, 18, 95, 158; Bob P.'s leadership of, 27, 28, 151; conciliatory approach of, 162-63; lack of opinions of, 161

Adams, Mary Louise, 147-48

Adler, Alfred, 13, 14-15, 107, 161

African-Americans, in AA, 162

Agnostics, in AA, 146, 159

Akron, Ohio: AA in, 29, 37, 61-62, 67-76, 114; Oxford Group meetings in, 67-71, 73; Oxford Group rally in, 65-67; split between AA and Oxford Group in, 89, 91, 93-94

Alcoholic Foundation, 75, 76, 143

Alcoholics Anonymous (AA): alternatives to, 159-61; beginnings of, 1, 11, 14, 15-26, 61-62, 67-76, 89-90; boosters of, in the modern church, 143-53; break of, with the Oxford Group, 27-28, 41, 89-99; coincidences, or synchronicity, in history of, 10, 14, 15, 26, 92, 103, 117; comparison of, to other organizations, 57, 161; cooperation of, with other organizations, 7-8, 168; criticism of, 2, 157-159; importance of spirituality in, 2-8, 133-34; importance to, of Bill Wilson's spiritual experience, 78, 86-87; in

Akron, 29, 37, 61-62, 67-76, 114; influence on, of evangelistic leaders, 127-141; influence on, of Frank Buchman and the Oxford Group, 6, 18, 28-32, 35, 38, 41-42, 45, 66, 67, 97, 138, 144; influence on, of medical profession, 119, 158; influence on, of Richard Peabody, 117-120, 123, 125; influence on, of Sam Shoemaker, 29, 51, 52, 55, 56, 58-59; in tradition of mutual self-help associations, 101-116; mission of, 167-72; principles and practices of, 6, 20, 51, 85, 92-93, 107, 109; status of, today, 2, 76, 155-65; synthesis of ideas in, 7, 115. *See also* International conferences, of AA

Alcoholics Anonymous. See Big Book, the

Alcoholics Anonymous Comes of Age, 11

Alcoholics for Christ, 160, 161

Alcoholics Victorious, 160

Alcoholism, 70-71, 140, 146, 161, 167; approach to, in Oxford Group, 37, 41, 66, 91; concern about, among evangelists, 130-34, 137, 140; help for, at Calvary Mission, 53-54; overcoming, 81, 86-87, 108-9, 130, 131-34; theories of, 6, 7, 16, 119; treatment of, by Richard Peabody, 16, 117-20, 123-24; treatment of, in Emmanuel Movement, 121-23

Alexander, Jack, 28, 61, 97

Allen, James, 105

Allergy theory. *See* Alcoholism

Amos, Frank, 61, 75-76

Founders Day anniversary (of AA), 69

Four Absolutes, the, 21, 64, 139; Bill Wilson's view of, 95, 138; emphasis on, in Akron AA, 76, 138; emphasis on, in Oxford Group/MRA, 41, 98

Four Absolutes, The, 138

Fox, Emmet, 5, 105, 106, 111-14

Fox, George, 34

Francis, Saint, 34, 149

Franklin, Benjamin, 101

Freud, Sigmund, 13, 15, 17, 107; opinion of, regarding religious conversion, 14; use of reason by, 161. *See also* Psychoanalysis

Fundamentalism, religious, 141, 144-45, 150, 153. *See also* Evangelism

G

G., Cebra (AA member), 19, 20, 26

Gammeter, John, 73

General Service Board (of AA), 162

General Service Conference (of AA), 45

General Service Office (of AA), 7-8

Gilliland, William, 35-36

God. *See* Higher Power

God Calling, 36-37

Gorbachev, Mikhail, 114

Graham, Billy, 58, 113, 134, 153

Great American Depression, 112

Guldseth, Mark O., 33, 135-36, 137

H

H., Charles (son of Rowland H.), 16

H., Rowland: consultation of, with Carl Jung, 10-18, 21, 165; recovery of, in Oxford Group, 11, 14, 18-19; sponsorship of Ebby T. by, 19-22, 25-26, 37

Hadley, Harry, 52-54, 128, 130

Hadley, Henry Harrison II. *See* Hadley, Harry

Hadley, S.H., 52-53, 128, 130

Harper's magazine: article in, about AA, 157-58; article in, about Carl Jung, 17

Harris, Irving, 48

Hartford Seminary, 37, 139

Higher Power, 24, 124, 140; Bill Wilson's relationship with, 78, 85, 86; importance of, in AA, 2, 109; in New Thought, 106; nature of, in AA, 4-6, 83, 146-47, 156, 159, 160, 161-62, 163-64

Hirschhorn, Joe, 115

Hitler, Adolf, 28, 30, 96

Homosexuals, in AA, 163

Hotel Thayer meeting, 89, 90-91

House parties, 38-39, 89

Howard, Peter, 98

How to Stay Sober: Recovery Without Religion (Christopher), 159

How to Win Friends and Influence People (Carnegie), 114-15

Huber, Richard M., 109, 110

Humanists, 158-59

Hunter, T. Willard: 27, 70n; comments of, on Frank Buchman, 18, 31, 34, 35, 44, 50, 57, 91

I

I Ching, 11

In Darkest England and the Way Out (Booth), 130-31

Indians, in AA. *See* Native Americans, in AA

International conferences, of AA, 44; in 1950, 6, 93; in 1955, 3, 51, 150, 167; in 1985, 168

In Tune with the Infinite (Trine), 105, 111

Isaiah, 82

J

J., Dan (AA member), 156

James, William, 24, 34, 81, 131, 133, 152, 153, 161; on "mind-cure," in *The Varieties of Religious Experience*, 104, 105; on Richard Bucke, in *The Varieties of Religious Experience*, 77-78, 79-80; on S.H. Hadley, in *The Varieties of Religious Experience*, 52, 130; on the Emmanuel Movement, in *The Varieties of Religious Experience*, 120

Jesuits, 144, 149-50

Jesus Christ, 82, 145, 152, 160, 161; Bill Wilson's view of, 88; in Frank Buchman's spiritual experience, 33-34; in *The Man Nobobdy Knows*, 110-11; in *The Sermon on the Mount*, 111-12

Jews, in AA, 146, 157

Jung, Carl, 107, 133, 161; consultation of, with Rowland H., 10-18, 21; influence of, on AA, 7, 18; response of, to Bill Wilson's letter, 10, 11-13, 18, 165

K

K., Kit (AA member), 156

Keswick Convention, 32-35, 48, 83, 136

Key person strategy, 30, 35, 66

Kurtz, Ernest, 134

L

Law of Reversed Effort, 108

Lawrence, Brother, 84, 106

Lean, Garth, 33, 57, 97

Litchfield, Paul, 66

Lord's Prayer, the, 157

Low, Abraham, 149

Loyola, Ignatius, 149-50

Luther, Martin, 34

Lutheran church, 32, 50

M

McAuley, Jerry, 52, 128-130, 161

McCarthy, Katherine, 121, 122, 123, 124, 125

McComb, Samuel, 120-21, 125

McKenney, Ruth, 50

McPherson, Aimee Semple, 113

Man Nobody Knows, The (Barton), 110-11, 112

Man the Unknown (Carrel), 7

Marble Collegiate Church, 113, 144, 150, 152

Masons, the, 148

Mayflower Hotel (Akron), 63, 65, 72

Medical profession, 2, 117; influence of, on AA, 6, 7, 119, 158

Mello, Nancy K., 7

Mendelson, Jack H., 7

Metaphysics, 152

Meyer, F.B., 32, 33

Modernism, religious, 141, 143-45, 147, 150, 153

Mohammed, 82

Moody, Dwight L., 33, 139, 140-41, 161; influence of, on AA, 128, 134, 136-38, 140, 144; spiritual experience of, 34, 82; theological views of, 141, 144-45

More Twice-Born Men, 39-40, 42, 92, 93, 132

Moral Re-Armament (MRA), 58, 66, 152; controversy associated with, 97; distancing of AA from, 28, 31; evolution of Oxford Group into, 44-45, 66, 91-92, 94, 97; mission of, 44, 57, 91-92, 169, 170; status of, today, 45, 98. *See also* Oxford Group

Moses, 82

Other titles that will interest you. . .

Not-God
A History of Alcoholics Anonymous
  by Ernest Kurtz, Ph.D.
  Thorough, comprehensive, and candid, this is the story of
Alcoholics Anonymous. Ernest Kurtz documents the history of
A.A., placing the development of the fellowship within the larger
framework of a changing America. In *Not-God,* Kurtz creates both
an absorbing story and a compelling historical work. 436 pp.
Order No. 1036

A Program for You
A Guide to the Big Book's Design for Living
  With down-home honesty, humility, and humor, this book
leads you through a meaningful study of *Alcoholics Anonymous,* the
Big Book. Its careful annotations and explanations help you under-
stand the design for living sought after and worked at by A.A.'s
founders and early members, a design that still works today. 179 pp.
Order No. 5122

A Skeptic's Guide to the Twelve Steps
  by Phillip Z.
  This is Phillip Z.'s story of coming to believe in a Power greater
than himself through the Twelve Step fellowship of Overeaters
Anonymous. This book is a beacon of reassurance for the recovering person in any Twelve Step fellowship who has questioned the
traditional Judeo-Christian concept of God, or has struggled to
believe in a Higher Power. 275 pp.
Order No. 5130

**For price and order information, or a free catalog,
please call our Telephone Representatives.**

HAZELDEN EDUCATIONAL MATERIALS

1-800-328-9000	**1-612-257-4010**	**1-612-257-2195**
(Toll Free. U.S., Canada, and the Virgin Islands)	(Outside the U.S. and Canada)	(FAX)

Pleasant Valley Road • P.O. Box 176 • Center City, MN 55012-0176